STAYING
ONE
STEP
AHEAD

TOM CZYZ

STAYING ONE STEP AHEAD

ENDING THE STORY OF ACTIVE SHOOTER IN AMERICA'S SCHOOLS

Advantage | Books

Published by Advantage, Charleston, South Carolina.
Member of Advantage Media.

ADVANTAGE is a registered trademark, and the Advantage colophon is a trademark of Advantage Media Group, Inc.

Printed in the United States of America.

10 9 8 7 6 5 4 3 2 1

ISBN: 979-8-89188-043-6 (Paperback)
ISBN: 979-8-89188-044-3 (eBook)

Library of Congress Control Number: 2024911537

Cover and layout design by Lance Buckley.

This publication is designed to provide accurate and authoritative information in regard to the subject matter covered. It is sold with the understanding that the publisher is not engaged in rendering legal, accounting, or other professional services. If legal advice or other expert assistance is required, the services of a competent professional person should be sought.

Advantage Media helps busy entrepreneurs, CEOs, and leaders write and publish a book to grow their business and become the authority in their field. Advantage authors comprise an exclusive community of industry professionals, idea-makers, and thought leaders. Do you have a book idea or manuscript for consideration? We would love to hear from you at **AdvantageMedia.com**.

DEDICATION

To all the school active shooter victims and their families, your strength and resilience in the face of unspeakable tragedy serve as a profound inspiration. It is my unwavering commitment to End the Story of Active Shooter and to work toward a future where no one else has to endure the pain and suffering that you have experienced.

To my wife, Maria, you have stood by my side and supported me on this journey and been my rock during the darkest moments when I struggled with my own PTSD from these tragic events. I hate the time we spend apart because of this mission, but I love that you are waiting for me every time I come home. Your patience, love, and even financial support during the hard times of growing a business have been lifesaving, and I am forever grateful to you. You are my world. I would not have had the success I have had without you. You are my soulmate and the love of my life.

To my children—Bailey, Noah, Isaiah, McKenzie, Adalis, and Liam "Memo"—I started this company to protect you at your schools, and now we protect schools all over America. Your support and belief in the importance of this work drive me to continue striving for a safer world for all.

To my parents, Randy and Maryanne, who instilled in me the values of compassion and protection and were resolute in their love and support, even in my most challenging days. Your prayers and steadfast belief in me have been felt and made me into the man I am today.

To my big brother, Jeremy Czyz, you were taken from us too soon, and I wish you could have seen what Armoured One turned into. I do not doubt that you would be proud of everything your little B accomplished. I love you and miss you.

To my fellow police officers and deputies with whom I had the honor to serve, the bond of brotherhood we forged will always be cherished. To my brothers in blue and for life, Jered Zeppetello, Mike Graham, and Laura Collins. Police work is hard, but having a friendship like ours has helped make our public service a fun and wild ride.

Lastly, I dedicate this book to my committed staff at Armoured One. Together, we are an army dedicated to eliminating evil from this world. Each of you plays a vital role in protecting America's schools, and I am honored to work alongside such a dedicated team. Regardless of your role at Armoured One, know that you are a crucial part of the team working toward a safer future for our children and communities.

Together, we will end the story of the active shooter.

CONTENTS

INTRODUCTION

More than anything, I wish this book didn't need to exist. I wish the work I do every day was unnecessary. But I only need to say a few words to explain why my work is needed:

Columbine.

Sandy Hook.

Parkland.

Uvalde.

Nashville.

And unfortunately, those are just a few of a long list of active school shootings. Not to mention active shooter attacks that have happened at military bases, grocery stores, churches, and even shopping centers.

Protecting people has always been a part of my DNA. My father was a pastor in the Assembly of God church. Not only did I watch him be a spiritual protector, but when 9/11 happened, he went of his own volition to Ground Zero to help in any way he could. I found my way to the specialized field of active shooter response after a nearly twenty-year career in law enforcement. This included work in homicide, SWAT, and learning everything I could about disrupting active shooter scenarios.

Sandy Hook is what changed everything for me.

On December 14, 2012, the world stood still as the news of the Sandy Hook Elementary tragedy unfolded. In my living room, I stood motionless as my TV narrated the unimaginable loss of twenty first graders and six staff members.

My eyes mirrored the despair gripping the nation as I listened to Kaitlin Roig (now Roig-DeBellis), a heroic teacher, share about how she protected fifteen children that day. With over a decade of law enforcement etched into my very being and a father's fierce instinct to protect his children, each horrifying detail from her story felt like a personal call to action.

As I went to Sandy Hook and conducted my own investigation, it became apparent that many of the same mistakes were being repeated—fixable mistakes which could have saved lives if only someone was leading the way in addressing the root issues. Which is where the idea for Armoured One came from. There *needed* to be an organization that could look at all sides of the situation, find the root of the problem, and stay one step ahead of an active shooter.

Ending the story of active shooter became very personal to me. Before she came to work for the company, my wife Maria was a city public school English teacher. Together, we have six kids whom we sent to school every day. I couldn't sit by with the thought of sending them to school, not knowing if I'd see them again.

We've envisioned a world where no parent would endure the torment of uncertainty about their child's safety at school. Armoured One was born, not just as a business but as a beacon of hope. Our primary mission is to save lives from an active shooter. To shield the innocent during the unthinkable, to turn schools into safe environments where children can learn, grow, and socialize. We carry this out by assessing the security needs necessary to protect K–12 students and staff across the nation.

Over the last decade, Armoured One has established itself as the nation's leading expert in school security. Our impact resonates globally, affecting over one hundred million lives in the past few years alone, a testament to our team's unwavering dedication to creating a safer world by staying one step ahead.

We've collected a diverse team of specialists, including former law enforcement officers, Homeland Security agents, Secret Service members, Special Forces operatives, SWAT operators, fire service professionals, engineers, architects, school staff, administrators, and more. This collective wisdom shapes our innovative solutions, ensuring that every safety measure we implement in schools is infused with real-world insights and proven effectiveness.

Our journey has had its share of hurdles. We've faced skepticism and government pushback, and the daunting scale of our mission has tested our own determination. Yet, with each challenge, our vision has become clearer, fueled by the stories of survivors, the determination of parents, and the resilience of communities. In the heart of Armoured One lies a simple driving truth: love.

We're driven by parents who want to protect their kids, by survivors who want to prevent pain for others. We're driven by people who want to make a difference and who want to save lives.

WHAT THIS BOOK IS

The purpose of this book is closely aligned with what we do every day at Armoured One. My greatest hope is for it to serve as a guide to know how your school should respond to active shooter scenarios before (prevention), during (response), and after (recovery).

In each of these areas, the shooting at Robb Elementary in Uvalde, Texas, will be a focal point. I chose Uvalde because it is an unfortunate case study in the mistakes we see repeated across schools, which then allows for the story of active shooter to continue.

This book will lay out solutions to these mistakes—practical actions every school and community can take to stay one step ahead of an active shooter. By doing so, we can create a safer world.

Throughout this book, there's an analogy I'd like you to keep in mind. Imagine you have a leaky roof. What are you going to do?

Would you call your local news weatherman to come take a look? How about your representative in Congress? Or what about your window guy—maybe some new energy-efficient windows will fix the leak?

Of course not. Either you'll ignore the problem and deal with the consequences when it caves in, or you'll call up a roofing expert to come out, assess the problem, find the problem, and then fix it.

For the past thirty years, though, this is the type of insanity cycle schools have been trapped in. They're taking cues from the media or government. They're taking the wrong actions, thinking it will fix the "leak in the roof." But sometimes, to find the leak, you've got to tear the shingles off. Until then, you're just guessing. And what happens if you guess wrong?

This book is designed to help you start tearing the shingles off to find where the "leak" in your school is—the vulnerabilities which can be exploited by an active shooter. As a guide, this is meant to be read from beginning to end. The later chapters will mean nothing to you if you have not digested the information at the beginning. That said, you'll also see some intentional repetition of concepts. Just like in a classroom, if you hear something said more than once, it's probably *really* important.

WHAT THIS BOOK ISN'T

On that note, I want to present a few of the Armoured One values which will also hold true for the information in this book.

First and foremost, if you're just looking for a checklist of products or trainings you want to fulfill to pacify a parents' group or government agency, this is *not* the book for you. This book is going to force you to reconsider your policies, your protocols, and your existing safety measures. It might make you realize you spent money on the wrong things. It might make you realize you haven't spent enough on the *right* things. It will challenge your preconceptions and compel you to act.

Second, this book is not a training manual for K–12 students. While we believe there is a place for training students for their response during a lockdown situation, this book is aimed at adults, those with the responsibility of keeping children safe at school. We will touch on this topic later on, but it needs to be stated now to prevent any misconceptions.

Third, we don't take any sponsorships for products. At Armoured One, our integrity comes first, so we'll never endorse a product we know to be inferior. Even if it's a product we like, we won't take a sponsorship or do a transactional endorsement. Part of our reasoning here is because companies and products change over time, but also, solutions should be tailor-fit to the school's specific safety needs.

We're not willing to stake our reputation on one product or company, even ones we like. Our recommendations to schools are based on what is best *now*—and this continues to change as new security measures and products become available. Therefore, you will not see many specific product recommendations here in the book—though I will warn you about some to avoid.

HURT AND HOPE

Also, I'll warn you now this book is *not* an easy read. Not because I use lots of fancy words—I assure you, I don't. But because there's a world of hurt behind the stories in these pages. I'm no stranger to PTSD myself, so it's only fair for me to warn you now that some of the information here could potentially be triggering for you.

Finally, I want to leave you with some hope. That's what this book is truly about. In the wake of a school shooting, it can feel like there's nothing you can do—especially when we see so much inaction from the government, and the media moves on to the next story. But you should have hope because *you* can take action. *You* can stay one step ahead of an attack. *You* can make the difference in ending the story of active shooter.

No one should live under a leaky roof. For one thing, it's miserable. More importantly, it's *dangerous*. When the storm hits, it will cave. But if you follow the advice in this book, you will be miles closer to creating the kind of school where children and staff are safe and will thrive.

My hope is that a day will come when this book is a relic. When it's no longer necessary. I pray that happens sooner rather than later.

|1|

DÉJÀ VU

Have you ever woken up and felt like something bad was going to happen? Something that had happened before—and now it's going to happen all over again?

On May 24, 2022, I had such a moment. The day felt different as soon as I woke up. It was a surreal moment of heightened awareness. Call it intuition, call it pessimism, call it the Holy Spirit, or call it BS—it's exactly how I felt.

"I feel like there's going to be a terrible shooting today," I told my wife Maria.

"Then, say your prayer," she advised me.

You hear a lot about prayers and thoughts being offered up *after* a school shooting has happened. I, for one, like to be more proactive. Nearly every day for almost ten years, I've started my workdays with a preemptive prayer of protection for schools:

"Lord, I pray protection over America's schools. I know that the devil is at work on some attacker's heart, and I pray against the lies being said to that boy. Turn him from his wicked thought of wanting to kill and put someone in his life to love and guide him. Protect our schools with your mightiest angels and get America's kids home to their families today."

I wish such prayers—whether before or after an event—were unnecessary. No matter what you believe, if you're reading this, I'm sure we can agree on that.

After breakfast, I headed to my office in the home we share together in Murrells Inlet, South Carolina. Maria headed down the hall to her office, where she works as president of ONE Training, a sister company of Armoured One.

Both companies were born out of the Sandy Hook school shooting in 2012 and my own discovery of all that went wrong there. In the decade-plus since, Armoured One has gone on to become the nation's leading school security organization, specializing in preparation and response for active shooter situations at K–12 schools. Numerous times a week, I get notified of a possible shooting happening somewhere. Sometimes, it's multiple times a day. It's just "another day at the office" for me.

As a former homicide detective and SWAT team operator, I've developed instincts in my gut and collected some memories that I wish I never had. The horrible scenes police officers witness do nothing to keep our minds from racing to the worst possible scenario. In 2012, my wife was a city high school English teacher, with all of our six kids going to public schools every day. Add all this up, and I have more empathy—and fear—about active shooter situations than the average person. So yeah, you better believe I start my day with a prayer.

Maybe my "sixth sense" about shootings comes from those experiences—like stories you hear about mothers who have sensed their child was in danger on the other side of the country. But it was around 12:45 p.m. when I started getting texts and phone calls from my contacts with state and federal agencies about a possible active shooter situation unfolding in Uvalde, Texas.

I had no idea where Uvalde, Texas was. To be fair, Texas is massive. Before I turned to Google to discover where Uvalde was located or whether the reports were true, I added another prayer:

"God, *please* let the reports I'm hearing on the news of an active shooter at Robb Elementary be false. I ask for protection over those children, the staff, and their families. In Jesus's name, amen."

Then, I dug into Google search to find out what was truly going on in Uvalde. I couldn't get in touch with some key law enforcement in Texas, which immediately spiked my worry. If they are not answering their phones, it's a bad sign.

Next, I reached out to some active federal agents we work with.

"You got any information on Uvalde?"

"We can't confirm if anyone is injured or dead," they replied. "But we know shots *were* fired at an elementary school."

My heart immediately sank. My mind reverted to the Sandy Hook attack, where twenty first graders and six adults were killed in the tiny Connecticut town. Additional research on Google did nothing to settle my stomach because there were differing reports all over the news. Some outlets reported there was an active shooter with an unknown number of children dead. Another news source said it was a false report. The next news agency reported there were only people injured, while another said it was the worst school shooting in a decade.

Being in our South Carolina office meant I was about eight hundred miles from our headquarters in Syracuse, New York. I called up headquarters and spoke to our director of security assessments. He works with our subject matter experts who are spread across the US—a robust team made up of former law enforcement investigators, SWAT, FBI, Secret Service, Navy SEALs, Delta Force, and other special forces. They are still highly connected with their prior units, so we can typically gather accurate intel faster than a news agency. You name it, our team is somehow connected to someone somewhere.

I called Syracuse and asked if they could confirm anything. I asked. "I'm headed into an important meeting, but as soon as you can confirm what's happening in Uvalde, call me on my cell and interrupt. I need to know if this is a false report, if anyone has been injured, or if we've got another Sandy Hook on our hands."

To this day, I don't even know why I started that next meeting. I couldn't think of anything other than those kids at Robb Elementary.

As I was sitting in the meeting, my heart was racing. I remember feeling every beat. Every minute of the meeting had me wondering if a child's heart had stopped beating. Is this the minute that a parent is going to learn their child is never coming home? Is this the moment an aunt or uncle or grandparent will never see their little loved one again? Is a little elementary school student going to find out their best friend was killed in the classroom next door? Is there a husband or a wife sitting at home who's not going to hug and kiss their spouse because they were killed at work trying to protect our kids?

When the day began, that meeting was supposed to be the most important discussion of the day. But soon, it turned into the least important. I can't tell you a single thing that happened in it after I walked in. My mind was in Uvalde even though I had never been there. Those poor kids, those poor families, that poor community.

If something *had* happened, I knew it had to be over by now. On average, these attacks only last about eight minutes.

Eight minutes.

That's all the time it takes to devastate a family, a community, and a single child's life. Let that sink in.

At the time I'm writing this, I've been to over sixty K–12 school shootings in the past eleven years, including Sandy Hook and

Parkland. I have been to a community just like Uvalde so many times; I sadly knew exactly what that community was experiencing. It keeps happening over and over and over again.

The story of the active shooter is a type of déjà vu our culture is experiencing. These kind of targeted school attacks have been happening since the 1970s, and yet we keep letting them happen. The political discourse of "solutions" only makes this insanity cycle worse. Each side becomes more entrenched in their own views instead of taking real action that can protect and save lives.

It's like finding out you've got a leak in your roof, but instead of fixing it, you ignore it completely. Then, you wonder why it caves in during the next storm. Or instead of calling a roofing expert for an inspection, you call up your local weatherman, or your representative in Congress. Not saying they aren't fine people, but what can they *actually* do about your roof?

To take the analogy further, maybe you *do* call a contractor—but you ask them to just install some new windows and doors, thinking this will somehow stop the leak. Believe me, I know this sounds ridiculous—but this is essentially how schools have been treating active shooter situations for over three decades now.

But unlike most déjà vu, we can stop this if we choose. There are real-life, practical steps that schools, law enforcement, and individuals can take which can bring an end to the story of the active shooter. We can't stop someone from wanting to do harm, from pulling the trigger of a gun any more than we can stop the rain. But we can have our roof inspected by a qualified professional. We can make sure there are no leaks. Likewise, we can—and must—do a better job of protecting our schoolchildren and teachers.

We don't have to be powerless before this awful déjà vu. We don't have to settle for a "leaky" roof. We can learn from the past and do better. We can look backward to know how to move forward. But we still have to make the personal choice to do so. It was the choice I made back in 2012.

So, let's focus on the real actions we can take to stay one step ahead of an active shooter. That is, the specific steps you can take to increase your security, improve your crisis responses, and protect your children and communities.

A CASE STUDY IN MISTAKES

My life was changed on that horrible day when Sandy Hook Elementary was attacked by a murderous twenty-year-old, whose own father later called him "evil."[1] At that time, I had been a police officer for over eleven years, and I was just starting my new role as a homicide detective, working for a sheriff's department in upstate New York.

From what I'd learned, I knew more needed to be done to stop an active shooter and to help school staff and students survive these vicious attacks. But our agency wasn't the size of the NYPD, LAPD, or Miami PD. We didn't have a full-time SWAT team. And given the fact most mass school shootings happen in towns with populations under seventy-five thousand,[2] what could we do to keep a Sandy Hook–type attack happening to the community we had sworn to serve and protect?

Solving this problem was "extra work" added to my job since I was now part of the Major Crime Unit in the Criminal Investigations Division. My life was becoming chaotic because of my new role

---

1   Andrew Solomon, "The Reckoning," *New Yorker*, March 10, 2014, accessed January 2, 2024, https://www.newyorker.com/magazine/2014/03/17/the-reckoning.

2   Lisa Marie Pane, "Mass School Shootings Mostly Happening in Small-Town America," Associated Press News, May 22, 2018, accessed January 2, 2024, https://apnews.com/article/8660507c56b04dd0b580b248d39d2a2c.

and then SWAT training added even more to my plate. Without a dedicated SWAT team, I had to wear both hats—homicide taking up most of my time. But the condition was if a SWAT situation arose, it *always* took priority.

In the early 2000s, at the beginning of my law enforcement career, I went to an active shooter training course. The instructor was Lt. Colonel Dave Grossman, who is one of the nation's leading experts on active shooters, an incredible instructor, a devoted father, and a man who loves God. After retiring from the army, it was a natural step for him to teach others about how to respond in a crisis situation where bullets are flying.

His class opened my eyes to the world of active shooters and how police needed to act like sheepdogs. That is, we have a sworn duty to protect the sheep—our kids, our school staff—who are herded to a school and then attacked by a hungry, ruthless wolf. As sheepdogs, we were born to protect the sheep—even at the cost of our own lives.

After Lt. Colonel Grossman's class, I attended every single course that was available about active shooters. I read book after book not only to learn the responses but also to understand the psychology of the shooter. Police work doesn't pay much, and sometimes, I would literally pay out of my own pocket to go through a class. I wanted to be prepared and to be the best at active shooter response in case it ever happened near me, God forbid. Armed with this knowledge, I began teaching law enforcement how to save lives and stop the threat of active shooters.

Which brings us back to May 24, 2022.

I was still holding out hope Syracuse would say that we had bad information, that it was a false report. How many times in the past decade alone have we seen breaking news about a school in lockdown or a reported active shooter at a school? News choppers swirl above the school, and journalists tell us details are coming "at any moment," only to find out it was a false report.

Not this time, though, despite my prayers.

It was around 1:30 p.m. Eastern when I heard back from Syracuse headquarters. Part of me did not want to answer the phone. Before he even spoke, the feeling in my gut told me it was going to be terrible—that kids and staff at the school were dead.

"Hey, boss, it is not good," he said. "A male gunman was shooting into Robb Elementary from the backyard of the school with a rifle, and then he entered the back building that holds classrooms. Police are on scene, and word is that the shooter is *still* in a classroom with hostages. People are reporting hearing a lot of gunshots."

It was a confirmed nightmare at Robb Elementary. It was more horrific than the media knew. There were at least twenty staff and students killed and many more injured. It was time for us to get on the move.

It's been our practice whenever there's a school shooting to get on-site as fast as we can. Since I couldn't catch a flight that evening, I was on the earliest one the next morning, headed to Texas. After landing, it was a ninety-minute drive before I was standing in front of Robb Elementary in Uvalde.

You might wonder why we don't wait for an invite from law enforcement or other officials. Well, to be frank, it's because if we were to wait for an invite, it would never come.

Some might feel like this is meddling. But what about the onslaught of media that shows up after a school shooting, shoving microphones into the faces of grieving parents? How are they helping the situation? As an organization filled with former law enforcement, we go so we can support their work and help them untangle the devastation. It's not unusual for them to have a shortage of both manpower and experience when it comes to school shootings.

In the days to follow, we would be part of the process of untangling the rumors and evidence to discover the truth of what had happened. I'd speak with law enforcement—local, state, and federal—assisting with the investigation. I'd speak with—and cry with—parents who had lost their children. In the investigative process, I would even speak with the Uvalde shooter's grandfather.

While each person I spoke to had their unique perspective, Uvalde itself was not unique in the story of active shooter. It was a painfully clear case of déjà vu. A tragic recycling of the same mistakes, the same dead-end conversations, and the deadly cycle of both inaction and taking the *wrong* actions.

Which is why Uvalde is a textbook case for us to consider. It's a case study in mistakes made before, during, and after the shooting. Yes, I'll touch on other school shootings and what we've learned from them—including attacks predating Columbine in 1999. But Uvalde will be the focal point because it has a lot to teach us if we will just be brave enough to look at it, learn from it, and then take the right actions. *That's* how we stay one step ahead of an active shooter so our children can be safe.

Until we can cut through the noise of politics, media talking heads, and bad assumptions, we'll keep making these same mistakes. We'll keep having the kind of déjà vu which allows the story of active shooter to write another painful chapter. Until we address these mistakes, nothing will change.

RESPONSIBILITY

It took one person making one terrible decision, and the entire Uvalde community was destroyed for probably a lifetime. Twenty-one precious lives were taken, seventeen more were injured, and thousands were wounded in their hearts and souls. These kids were supposed to be safe at school—but they were not.

In the aftermath, everyone wants to know who's responsible. Is it the school's fault, the state's fault, the federal government's fault, or law enforcement's fault?

Based on what I saw in Uvalde, I'd say "yes" to all of these. There's never one single point of blame, though our investigation would uncover who was *primarily* at fault. The greatest cause was the shocking lack of response and urgency from the local police—a finding which ended up being supported by the US Justice Department's own Uvalde report.[3]

In the end, we all have to confront our own responsibility. We all have a responsibility to stay one step ahead of the next attack. That's true if you're a school administrator, a teacher, a cop, an EMT, a parent, or the citizen who lives across the street from the school. This story has happened so many times. We know the patterns, we know the mistakes that get made, and we know what works and what doesn't work. But we have to take responsibility to address those mistakes.

That's where the rest of this book will take us. The actions which we can responsibly take before, during, and after an active shooter attack. If we can get good enough at the *before* and *during* pieces, then we won't have to deal with the *after* part. As crazy as it sounds to some, I'd love nothing more than for us to go out of business.

By the end of this book, I want you to have the confidence and clarity to take real action in your school and community to end the story of active shooter. The first step is to confront the false confidence

---

3   Brandon Drenon, "US Justice Department Says 'Lack of Urgency' Led to Failed Response to Uvalde Shooting," BBC News, January 18, 2024, accessed April 8, 2024, https://www.bbc.com/news/world-us-canada-68020254.

and confusion that result from the myths and bad assumptions you have about active shooter scenarios.

These myths and assumptions are the most likely to compromise your sense of responsibility. Before entering this line of work, I had my own bad assumptions I had to untangle. My own objections I had to resolve. Nothing in the rest of this book will matter if you can't do the same.

If you've already read this far, then it's safe to assume you're ready for change. You're ready for real action. Otherwise, what's to stop the déjà vu from coming to you? What's to stop your school and your community from becoming the next Uvalde?

2

MYTHS AND
ASSUMPTIONS

After Sandy Hook, I really thought the fight for school safety would only be against active shooters. I thought, *Maybe now, we'll finally see action and finally see proven safety measures put in across the board.*

I was wrong.

I assumed it would be easy to unify school administrators, law enforcement, parents, and politicians to agree that our schools needed to be hardened, properly trained, and armed with a school resource officer (SRO). I thought schools and law enforcement would be given more access to licensed counselors to help with our nation's surging mental health crisis.

The hard truth is that not much has changed. Some of the rhetoric has changed. Technology has changed. But the underlying problems have not been dealt with. I thought within ten years after Sandy Hook, we would make great strides to end the story of active shooters.

Uvalde proved otherwise. We're still seeing the same problems. Why?

What I've seen time and again is that the root of all the problems lies in the collective myths and bad assumptions people believe when it comes to school safety. These myths and assumptions keep us one step *behind* attackers. Which is why we need to start there. You can't build a safe school on a cracked foundation. And these myths keep us from having safe schools.

Fair warning—many of the topics addressed here will challenge preconceptions you may have about school safety and active shooter scenarios. Whether you vote Red, Blue, Green, or anything in between, you'll likely find a myth here which could rile you. But if your child was running out into a busy street—and you're too far away to catch them yourself—you're not going to care *who* saves them. You won't stop to ask them if they're Republican, Democrat, Christian, Muslim, or an Atheist. If someone saves your child's life, you'll be forever grateful, period.

Wherever I go, I ask school administrators the same question: "What is your number one job?" Nearly every time, I hear the same response: "To educate children."

I consistently challenge this mindset. The purpose of school is to keep children safe and alive. Nothing else can happen otherwise. Math, science, sports—none of it can happen if there is no foundational purpose of safety. Education is an *outcome* of schools when safety is in place.

When your primary purpose is safety, it makes you a better educator. Because now you're no longer concerned with a mere test score or assignment; you're thinking about a student's emotional safety, psychological safety, and intellectual safety. Don't take it from me; take it from researchers who are smarter than me, such as Harvard University's Center on the Developing Child:

"For young children who perceive the world as a threatening place, a wide range of conditions can trigger anxious behaviors that then impair their ability to learn and to interact socially with others."[4]

In other words, if a school says they care about education, then they cannot disregard safety. This should be obvious, yet time after time, I see schools make decisions they know are unsafe—or ignore the evidence and expertise provided to them—because safety is not a priority. With this in mind, let's dive into the biggest myths and assumptions about school safety and active shooters.

MYTH #1: ACTIVE SHOOTERS DO WHAT THEY DO BECAUSE THEY WERE BULLIED

We're going to come right out of the gate with one of the biggest bad assumptions I see—that the main reason active shooters go on their rampages is because they were bullied.

I was once asked by the Virginia Department of Criminal Justice to attend an event and speak to a crowd of around a thousand school leaders and law enforcement. During the Q and A portion, someone brought up a question which I hear nearly every time I speak about active shooters and school safety. In general, the question goes like this:

"Isn't it true that bullying is the real issue here?"

Often, they are referring to what they are seeing on the news or various government reports. The finger is being pointed at bullying as the true villain.

---

4   National Scientific Council on the Developing Child, "Persistent Fear and Anxiety Can Affect Young Children's Learning and Development, Working Paper 9," Center on the Developing Child at Harvard University, 2010, 3, https://developingchild. harvard.edu/wp-content/uploads/2010/05/Persistent-Fear-and-Anxiety-Can-Affect-Young-Childrens-Learning-and-Development.pdf.

The tough part of this myth is, like many myths, there is some truth in it. Bullying is definitely part of the problem, but it's not the primary problem. Whenever I'm asked this question, I typically address the entire room and say, "If you've never been bullied ever—by a classmate, an older sibling, a cousin, a coworker, a neighbor—can you raise your hand?"

No one ever raises their hand. It doesn't matter if you're Hulk Hogan, six-foot-seven, and three hundred pounds of muscle. At some point, someone in your life has been bigger than you—or been in a position of power over you—and has bullied you. For crying out loud, even as an adult, I've had contractors try to bully me!

What makes this a myth is that, while bullying is a factor in someone becoming an active shooter, it's not the only one. Otherwise, we'd have even more mass shootings than what we see. The insinuation of this myth is, "Active shooters aren't bad people; they're hurt people."

My stance is that these don't have to be mutually exclusive. A hurt person can also choose to turn their hurt into a force for good—and many do. It comes down to personal choice. We don't need to justify an active shooter's behavior. I have all the compassion in the world for someone who is hurting and needs help. But once they decide to pull a trigger, once they decide to hurt someone, the time for compassion is over, and it's time to take action.

If we start justifying criminal behavior by blaming bullying, there's no end in sight to the slippery slope. Will we let rapists off the hook because they were sexually assaulted themselves? Of course not. Let's not defend abusers.

The problem is when bullied people take their hurt and turn it into vengeance. Case after case, when you look into the writings left behind by active shooters, you see the same trend. Most of the active shooters want to be face-to-face with their victims—often because they want some type of godlike control over someone else's life. They want to see their victims in fear or begging for their lives.

We shouldn't discount the infamy factor either. As a company, our policy is to never say the shooter's name because these shooters *want* to go down in infamy. They want you to know their name and face forever. We take this power away by calling them a shooter, suspect, or attacker. It was no accident the shooters at Columbine chose April 20—Adolf Hitler's birthday. It was no accident the shooter at a recent incident in Iowa played the same music as the Columbine shooters. They are looking to be remembered in any way they can be.

It all comes down to a personal choice made by the active shooter. It comes down to a choice to *be evil*. People balk when I use the word *evil*, but what else would you call it when someone takes so many lives in such a calculated way? Some of these active shooters have more victims than infamous serial killers—the difference is the serial killers conducted their evil acts over a longer course of time and hid their acts.

As difficult as this is, think for a moment about the shooter in Parkland. It was Valentine's Day 2018, where the attacker walked into Marjory Stoneman Douglas High School, Building 12, wielding an AR15. He walked into the hallway and immediately killed three of his victims and injured one more. This was just the beginning of his rampage. He continued his massacre and shot some of his victims until they were *unrecognizable*. Even when they were already dead, he continued to shoot them.

It was the same in Uvalde where the medical examiner's reports showed the shooter continued to shoot the dead bodies, nearly decapitating them. Parents had to identify their children by the clothes and shoes they were wearing because faces were gone. This is *far* beyond the actions of someone who was bullied and is acting out of self-preservation.

You don't even see this kind of violence in nature. If a mama bear's cubs are attacked, she goes into full protective mode. Once the attacking animal is dead or injured, the mama bear walks away. She doesn't continue to rip apart the attacking animal out of punishment, anger, or hatred. What we see from the attackers at Columbine, Red Lake, Sandy Hook, Parkland, and Uvalde is pure evil and hate.

During our work in Uvalde, I sat down with the shooter's own grandfather, who is a sweet, Christian man. He told me about all he'd tried to do to help his grandson for years, how he had loved him, and how the shooter wouldn't take any of his help. On the morning of the shooting, the shooter tried to kill his own grandmother. The grandfather had tears in his eyes when he told me, "He was just pure evil that day."

Should we be tackling the problem of bullying in our schools? Absolutely! Doing so is also part of keeping kids safe in school. No child should be afraid to go to school. No teacher should be afraid to go to work. But it would be a fool's errand to believe that eradicating all bullying will also eradicate shootings. Calling shooters "evil" is not a scapegoat to let them off the hook—they still need help and intervention before the shooting.

We need to tackle bullying beyond *stopping* it. We need to find out the *why* behind it. We need to find out what's happening at home, or if a bullied child needs resources or counseling. Maybe they feel isolated or ignored. With compassion, we need to help these kids while we still can—*before* some of them decide to take matters into their own hands.

MYTH #2: "SCHOOL SHOOTINGS ARE A NEW PROBLEM"

When we discuss school shootings, most people go back to Columbine as the starting point. We arbitrarily draw a line at 1999 to say, "Here's where it all started." But this simply isn't true.

When I took Lt. Colonel Grossman's course on Identifying and Stopping Active Killers, it opened my eyes to a history I never knew. He shared with us about the first documented school shooting in the US—the Enoch Brown school massacre in 1764, located in modern-day Franklin County, Pennsylvania. You read that right—school shootings predate our nation's independence.

At this point in history, the colonists were frequently at war with Native Americans. This was just after the French and Indian War, where the French had been arming local Native tribes against their common enemies—the Brits. But the French had called it off and surrendered the year before. The Native Americans were still armed—and angry they had lost their allies in their bid to reclaim land from the British.[5]

On July 26, 1764, four members of the Delaware Lenape tribe decided to take vengeance on the local settlers who were still under British rule at the time. They realized the log schoolhouse was vulnerable—with only one adult present, the schoolmaster Enoch Brown. When the warriors entered, he pleaded with them for the safety of the children—and then he was shot, beaten, and scalped in front of the children.

The attackers then turned their wrath upon the small group of children—eleven in total—and killed all save one. The one survivor,

---

5   Bill Hand, "The First School Shooting Was in 1764," *New Bern Sun Journal*, September 29, 2018, accessed via archive February 10, 2024, https://web. archive.org/web/20180929233518/http://www.newbernsj.com/news/20180406/ first-school-shooting-was-in-1764.

Archie McCullough, was scalped himself but was able to then hide in a fireplace and escape to a creek to clean his wounds.

It should be noted that this attack does not truly reflect the ways of the Lenape people. Their chief later denounced the four warriors, calling them cowards for attacking children. Despite the harm done to his people by the settlers, he did not justify the attackers in their evil actions.

Unfortunately, other accounts of school attacks can be found going back nearly a hundred years. In Bath, Michigan, in 1926, the school board treasurer was angry about his taxes and losing the election for township clerk. When he was notified that his house would also be foreclosed on, it was the final straw, and he hatched a plan for revenge.

After purchasing explosives during the following months, he secretly packed Bath Consolidated School with bombs—and killed thirty-eight children and six adults on May 18, 1927. Another fifty-eight people were injured in the explosion, rocking the small community. And as a precursor to what we see all too often, he also set off a bomb at his own home, killing his wife, though he killed himself in the second explosion at the school.[6]

We begin to see more patterns of modern active shooter incidents in cases like the Cleveland Elementary School shooting in San Diego, California, on January 29, 1979. In that case, a sixteen-year-old female used a rifle from her home to take aim at children inside the elementary school across the street. She ended up wounding eight children as well as killing the principal Burton Wragg, teacher Daryl Barnes, and custodian Mike Suchar—all of whom were trying to get the children to safety. Police were able to prevent additional casualties, reportedly by moving a garbage truck in front of the school entrance to obstruct her shots.

---

6   The full story and details can be found in *Bath Massacre: America's First School Bombing* by Arnie Bernstein, published by University of Michigan Press, 2009.

When a reporter got in touch with the shooter while she was barricaded inside her home, the reason she gave for her attack was, "I don't like Mondays. This livens up the day." Unfortunately, this statement went on to inspire a popular song, showing how easy it is for the media to glorify such horrific acts, which only goes on to inspire additional attacks.

On September 8, 1988, a nineteen-year-old male stole his grandmother's .22 caliber handgun and proceeded to Oakland Elementary School in Greenwood, South Carolina. Once he arrived, he opened fire inside the cafeteria, injuring one teacher and three students. The attacker left the cafeteria and entered the girls' restroom to reload when physical education teacher, Kat Finkbeiner, fought with the suspect to try to stop him. During the struggle, she was shot in the head and the hand.

The attacker then entered a classroom, where he opened fire again, injuring five students and killing one. Somehow after being shot in the head, Finkbeiner summoned the strength to approach the shooter *again* and help restrain him until police arrived. Once his gun was emptied, he dropped it and exited the school, where police apprehended him.[7]

In all these cases, we begin to see trends for active shooter cases—individuals moved by vengeance, rage, and in some cases, untreated mental illness and past abuse. We shouldn't be surprised when we see these same motives in today's active shooters—which is why it's all the more important we prioritize safety in schools. Staying one step ahead includes taking preventative actions like identifying at-risk individuals so they can be properly treated and cared for, as well as implementing safety measures which prevent a shooter from being able to access children and staff during an attack.

---

7   Mary Brooks, "Gunman Opens Fire in School," *Washington Post*,
     September 27, 1988, accessed March 11, 2024, https://www.washington-
     post.com/archive/politics/1988/09/27/gunman-opens-fire-in-school/
     cfce70d0-8b64-40ed-8553-9848a30ca37e/.

MYTH #3: "IT WON'T HAPPEN HERE"

I hear this myth far too often. Sometimes, I hear it from people at the scene of the crime—parents, school personnel, law enforcement, and community members. They often say, "I never thought this would happen here." In such times, my job is to show compassion and care as they grapple with the reality of the shooting.

The other time I hear this myth, unfortunately, is from school administrators and district board members. Too many times, I will hear someone say, "We don't need any of this. It won't happen here. Everyone knows everyone in our town. We all watch out for each other. We have a great relationship with law enforcement." And sometimes, they'll add on, "You're just making a sales pitch. We have other issues we need to take care of."

One time, I was called to consult a small school district in upstate New York. I was brought out by the superintendent because they had just had three middle school boys arrested for having weapons—and it was found the boys had planned to go to a school with the intent to kill. The only reason they failed was because a family member found out and reported them.

Despite the fact that they nearly had a school shooting, the school board looked at me and flat-out said, "This will never happen here." Five years later, though, we're finally working with them to beef up their protocols, training, and building safety.

During our work in Uvalde, we heard that the wife of one of the local police officers had been killed in the attack. My mind raced back to my worst nightmare—the fear of my own wife Maria dying in a school shooting back when she was a high school teacher. I used to literally wake up sweating after dreaming that Maria or one of our six kids were killed at school—all because I couldn't get there in time.

I am sure many of you have the same fear or nightmare. Unfortunately, this nightmare became a reality for Uvalde. Like every school active shooter community, the people there said the same thing: "I never thought this could happen here."

It's an easy myth to believe because you don't *want* to believe it could happen in your community. But the history of school shootings shows us it can happen anywhere—and as I mentioned in the first chapter, school shootings are actually *more* likely to occur in smaller communities.

If you're curious why that is, it comes down to resources. Large cities are more likely to have full-time police in a school, more robust programs for anti-bullying and mental health treatment, as well as more socialization for kids who would be ostracized in smaller towns.

For instance, imagine you're the one LGBTQ+ kid in a small town—you're getting picked on and probably not getting much in-person support. But in a large city, there's a whole club full of other people like you where you are embraced and where you have a positive outlet for your struggles.

None of us want to believe we'll ever have a bad car accident, but we still have auto insurance. No one wants to believe their house will ever burn down, but they still have fire insurance. While you can never guarantee a school shooting "won't happen here," you *can* take proactive steps to train your staff, improve your protocols, and use tools in your building's security setup to protect your students and staff.

MYTH #4: "SHOOTINGS ONLY HAPPEN IN PUBLIC SCHOOLS"

On March 27, 2023, a major myth was busted when an assailant entered Covenant School and murdered three students and three staff. Police arrived minutes later at the private school located in

Nashville and took down the shooter after the attacker refused to surrender to them.

It has long been assumed by parents and officials alike that private schools are inherently safer than public schools because they cater to a different "class" of students, so to speak. This has lulled many into a *false* sense of security, which is the *worst* kind of security.

While it's certainly true more school shootings occur at public schools, it's partly because there are more public schools than private. It's a sheer matter of volume. Since Columbine, around 5–7 percent of school shootings have happened in private schools. Yet, according to 2022 data, there are 15.8 million public high school students compared to 1.36 million private high schoolers.[8] That means, there's eleven times more high school students in public schools than private—not to mention private middle and elementary schools not included in the statistics.

You can't assume safety just because it's a private school. Nor can you assume safety in any other public venue. In 2015, my state of South Carolina was rocked by the news of the Emanuel AME Church shooting in Charleston, where nine people lost their lives. And it made headlines across the world when a shooter attacked a local grocery store in Buffalo, New York, on May 14, 2022, killing ten people and injuring others. During the investigations, both attacks were found to be racially motivated, once more underpinning that bullying is not the only issue we need to be concerned with if we are to end the story of an active shooter.

Active shooter situations aren't just a public school problem—which is why my initial training came from people like Lt. Colonel

---

8   Veera Korhonen, "Enrollment in Public and Private Schools in the United States in 2022," Statista, October 17, 2023, accessed February 12, 2024, https://www.statista.com/statistics/184010/school-enrollment-in-public-and-private-institutions-2008/.

Grossman. While most of our work at Armoured One is with public schools—once again, due to sheer volume—they're not the only organizations we work with. Private schools, churches, and any business with a high concentration of people can learn from the strategies detailed later in the book.

MYTH #5: "ANY PROTECTION IS BETTER THAN NO PROTECTION"

The idea that any protection is better than no protection is one of the deadliest on this list. It's evidence of a dangerous mentality I see among many school administrators and even law enforcement—treating school safety like a checklist of items. If you're going to protect your school, then you better do it the right way with the right protective measures—or you could end up in a worse situation.

Usually, the way I see this play out is when schools spend good money to install inferior equipment. Sometimes, they even know it's inferior, but as long as they can tell parents, "We have lockdown buttons," or, "We have bullet-resistant glass," they feel like they've done their job. But not all bullet-resistant glass will do the trick.

In fact, here's a bonus myth bust for you—there's no such thing as "bullet-*proof* products." What does exist is bullet-*resistant* products.

Recently, Tennessee passed a bill requiring public schools to install a type of window laminate that supposedly makes the existing windows bullet-proof. The only problem? The truth.

Like much of life, if it sounds too good to be true, it probably is. And that's exactly the case with many of these so-called "bullet-proof" products. True bullet-resistant glass is so thick (2.5 inches), it won't fit standard window frames. You have to re-engineer the windows themselves, which adds up to a considerable cost. As a result, most states aren't mandating such measures in their schools. Not even the FBI is using the right kind of glass yet. But you know who is? The Internal Revenue Service.

In Uvalde, the shooter started his attack outside the school building, shooting from the parking lot. While no one was killed from those shots, the bullets still penetrated the windows. Most walls aren't bullet-resistant either—bullets can go straight through sheetrock like it's paper. Most school administrators I meet aren't aware of the various grade levels for glass, so they simply don't think to ask vendors about it.

Unfortunately, there are other times where administrators *do* know about these grade levels for glass—but intentionally choose to forgo due to the higher cost. Instead, they go with the budget option so they can give people "peace of mind." They know the average parent isn't going to be asking them about glass grading. But if you're a parent—or any taxpayer—reading this, you *should* be asking. You don't want your tax dollars being spent on inferior products just so a box can get checked off. It's literally life and death.

Think about it this way: Imagine you have a sixteen-year-old daughter out on the road, and she gets a flat tire. You live in a rural area, and the cell service is nonexistent where she gets stuck. No one can get to her fast, and it's getting dark, so she's got to change her own tire. But when she opens up the trunk, all she finds is a spare *bicycle* tire.

Sure, it's a spare tire. But will it help her get to safety? Of course not. This "spare tire" mentality is what I see happening across many schools. Sometimes, it's happening out of ignorance. Other times, it's happening because they don't want to spend the time or money doing protection right. Which brings us to our next point …

MYTH #6: "WE CAN'T AFFORD PROTECTIVE MEASURES"

As I've said before, protection must be the priority. Consider the US government—regardless of your politics, its main role is to protect the people. It does this through the military, through enacting laws, and through the judicial system. It doesn't matter if you're the wealthiest nation in the world if you have no security and anyone can march in and take the place over.

The question I have for many schools is *very* unpopular: "Where are you prioritizing your money?" Look, I love sports. I played football in high school and still love the game. But when I see a school with a multimillion-dollar football stadium and they say they can't afford protective measures, it tells me the priorities are in the wrong place. What good is a state championship if someone can easily walk into your school, kill kids and staff, and leave an entire community grappling with PTSD?

It's fair to say this isn't the case with all schools. I've been to schools that want the protective measures but do not have the budget from the state. If we work together to make school safety a priority, if we put pressure on the politicians, we can create new funding for safer schools—we just need to make sure it's the right amount for the right protective measures.

Sometimes, I've heard the argument in board meetings that, "The taxpayers own the building. It's owned by the community." This argument is used to justify why they don't lock their doors and why they let anyone come into the school to use it. But the taxpayers of America technically own the White House, and we don't let just anyone walk into there, do we? The taxpayers own the money mints, but you can't just go in and take a handful, can you?

We need to see our schools the same way—not only to protect from active shooters but anyone else who would want to do harm to a child. Safety must come first. You can't educate without it. You can't have thriving sports without it. You can't have theater club, marching band, chess club, or any of the other extracurriculars without it.

We have to prioritize safety—in our minds and our budgets. You'll pay for it in the long run if you *don't* have the right protection in place. Case in point—the Parkland, Florida, shooting where the Department of Justice helped settle forty civil cases to the tune of $127.5 million.[9]

But more importantly, you cannot put a price tag on human life. Period.

MYTH #7: "ANY TRAINING WILL DO"

As you can imagine, this myth is closely related to the two before it. Schools often have a "get it done" mentality when it comes to training. The only thing worse is when they also have a "get it done for free" mentality.

It becomes clear where the true priorities are when you follow the money. I've personally seen schools pay top dollar—$300 a day per staff member—for their teachers to be trained in Common Core for ten days. You do the math. Yet, when it comes to training staff for security measures and lockdown situations? Schools will often settle for a single hour of training from anyone they can find.

Schools often make the misguided decision to rely on local police for such training. We'll get into this more in the next chapter, but

9   Office of Public Affairs, US DOJ, "Justice Department Announces Civil Settlement in Cases Arising from 2018 School Shooting in Parkland, Florida," Justice.Gov, March 16, 2022, accessed February 12, 2024, https://www.justice.gov/opa/pr/justice-depart-ment-announces-civil-settlement-cases-arising-2018-school-shooting-parkland.

the problem with doing so is that not all law enforcement officers (LEOs) are trained in active shooter response—or *certified* to train others. Remember, when I was in law enforcement myself, I had to get special training on the subject. Not only that, but sometimes, police officers can give well-intentioned but wrong advice. After all, they're thinking like a cop—not like a teacher who has to protect a classroom without a weapon.

To effectively train staff for an active shooter situation, you have to be able to think like a shooter. You have to know how they move—and how you should counter based on the exact analytics of your school's layout. That way your training can be a comprehensive plan based on proof of what has worked yet tailored to your school's exact situation.

Once again, Uvalde is an example of how dangerous this myth can be. During our investigation, as we spoke with witnesses and staff, we learned that the emergency response training done in the schools had been "Cold War" style training—teaching kids to hide under desks with their hands over their heads. Such tactics are completely ineffective in active shooter situations. They had also taught kids to "pretend to be dead." This is also bad training when you consider what we discussed early about attackers who continued to shoot dead bodies.

Just because someone has a badge and gun doesn't make them qualified to teach active shooter response. It might make them an expert in policing but not anything else. Think about it like specializations in the medical field—your dentist is an expert on teeth, not cancer treatment.

No different with school safety. Qualified trainers need to be following the FBI and Homeland Security–approved program "Run, Hide, Fight,"[10] and they need to become certified instructors before

---

10   FBI, "Active Shooter Safety Resources," FBI.gov, accessed April 4, 2024, https://www.fbi.gov/how-we-can-help-you/active-shooter-safety-resources.

they are teaching anyone what to do. In Uvalde, Chief Pete Arredondo had taken it upon himself to teach response in the schools, but he was not qualified to do so.

Speaking of, many schools have eliminated the "Run, Hide, Fight" training even though it's been the most effective strategy. They take issue with the word "fight" and see it as encouraging violence. They end up throwing out the entire strategy, despite its efficacy in saving lives. Instead, they need to look at the word "fight" in the same sense we would say "fighting cancer" or "fighting for your life." Because that's exactly what it teaches—fighting for your life, not senseless violence.

MYTH #8: "LAW ENFORCEMENT WILL ALWAYS BE THERE FOR US WHEN WE NEED THEM"

This one is particularly painful for me to address as former law enforcement myself. One bad assumption I've had to put in check is assuming everyone in law enforcement shares my values: hardworking and dedicated to the cause of protecting innocent people. In my mind, the ideal police officer has their work second only to their dedication to family and faith. Sadly, this isn't true for all police—or employees—though there are an overwhelming number of those who do share these values.

But like so much of life, nothing is ever 100 percent. We'll unpack this more in the next chapter, but sometimes, small communities get lulled into a sense of false security because the schools and police are so near to one another—both geographically and their personal relationships.

In one school, we were pushing the school board to get some SROs as additional security, but they didn't want to pay for it. Part of their justification was because the police chief at the time told the school board, "We're just a mile down the street. Someone is always at the station and can be there within one minute, no matter what."

When they later had a lockdown situation which I'll detail later, it also coincided with an especially terrible day for their police department. Not even the chief was in the office at the time of the lockdown—and it took eight minutes for police to arrive.

In Uvalde, though, we saw what might be the worst police response of all time. Information reached our New York office in the early afternoon that the shooter was still in the school even though the attack was believed to have started around 11:30 a.m. central time.

I initially assumed this information had to be a rumor or bad info. It sounded impossible. Even the shooters at Columbine committed suicide after about forty-five minutes. Keep in mind, that was back when police would *not* chase down a shooter but called the SWAT team to confront them.

Since then, we've largely learned our lesson as law enforcement—with the exception of the SRO's failure in the Parkland shooting. In that case, he did not enter Building 12 during the attack because he was both unprepared and scared to face the shooter. His inaction likely cost lives. Yet, even there, Parkland was over in about seven minutes once other law enforcement arrived.

But as our own investigation showed, backed up by the Department of Justice report, the police disregarded the generally accepted protocols for active shooter situations. Under the direction of Chief Arredondo, they retreated from gunfire and essentially abandoned the children and staff to fend for themselves against the armed shooter. It was over an hour from the start of the attack before off-duty Border Patrol agents entered the school to neutralize the shooter.

STAYING ONE STEP AHEAD

I wish I could say you can always depend on law enforcement to be there when you need them. That's the way it *should* be. They should be willing to lay down their lives—to serve and protect—as they've sworn to do. It's difficult for me to admit this one is a myth.

In the next chapter, we'll talk not only about how schools can be better prepared for active shooter situations, but how law enforcement can be better prepared. Later, we'll talk about the *correct* response—what will save children's lives, even if it means police end up laying down their own.

MYTH #9: "IT'S TOO SOON TO TAKE ACTION"

All too often, I see this myth play out in various ways—before, during, and after an active shooter situation. Often, it's said with good intentions and from a sense of caution. When it comes to active shooter situations, the balance between caution and action must go in whatever direction will protect lives.

Sometimes, Armoured One will be called in to assess the security needs of a school. We conduct a thorough inspection and then present our recommendations to the school board. Keep in mind, many of our recommendations are not even related to services we personally provide—such as the installation of lockdown systems. It's not unusual for me to hear some version of this myth in response to the costs: "It's too soon for us to take action on these recommendations. It's not in the budget."

This response fails to consider the ramifications—when a child dies at the hands of a shooter, it's too late. We have to accept there is no "perfect" time to get prepared. But it's never too soon.

Unfortunately, this is also the mentality we saw in the police response with Uvalde—saying it was too soon to go in and take action.

Chief Arredondo literally told his people and the SWAT Team not to go in while parents were screaming at them to do something. They didn't try a key on the door to get in, even though it was unlocked anyway—all because of the fear of taking fire, instead of being worried about the kids and staff inside.

When you've got an active threat on campus—whether they are inside or outside the building—it's never too soon to take action.

But where I hear this phrase the most is *after* the shooting has taken place. Some politicians will say it's "too soon to reopen the gun debate," all under the guise of letting people mourn. They know that enacting new laws and enforcing security measures will lose them votes.

One way this mentality plays out practically is a lack of resources for the grieving community. Their police forces are understaffed to handle the additional demands of investigation on top of the regular policing that needs to happen. All too often, these small communities don't have enough counselors, pastors, or medical personnel to deal with the aftermath.

I spoke with a family impacted by the Parkland shooting who told me about the trauma their autistic son was going through. He had actually seen the shooter, tried to communicate this information to his class, but wasn't believed. Then, because his mom had always told him to run away from danger, he got out of the building as fast as possible.

The boy was traumatized by the event, and yet, he was denied counseling. Florida was only providing support services to those who were injured or loved ones to the deceased. Because they couldn't get the help he needed, he later began using drugs to cope and even attempted suicide.

Instead, we need to treat these situations the way we do with natural disasters. After a major hurricane, FEMA rolls in with vans to provide additional resources to an entire community, whether their house was destroyed or not. Why would we not do the same to help these communities who just faced the unthinkable?

A good example of taking immediate action is when Governor Abbott of Texas stationed state police in Uvalde for an entire year to help provide additional law enforcement support and peace of mind. That's exactly the sort of fast action people need in the wake of such a horrible event.

A bad example of taking immediate action is when the Newtown Public School district told families they had to have their kids back in school the following Monday after the Sandy Hook shooting. *That* is too soon. And why? Because the district received state funding based on the number of days children were in school. At best, their mandate was completely inconsiderate of the community's needs.

Another bad example of taking fast action is when the community adopts a mob mentality and they want to see everyone fired right away—the police, the superintendent, the principal. In their hurt, they want someone to take the blame. There's nothing wrong with wanting justice. But it takes time to figure out what exactly went wrong—and who is to blame. It's dangerous to assign scapegoats.

In Uvalde, a lot of parents wanted Superintendent Harrell and the school board fired right away, ready to come after them with pitchforks. Were there actions they could have taken to better prepare the school? Yes. *Every* school board can be more proactive. We need minimum standards for training and security standards to address current gaps in the system. So many details are ignored which would be simple to fix—and save lives.

MYTH #10: "IT'S A MENTAL HEALTH PROBLEM, NOT A GUN PROBLEM"

Keeping kids safe shouldn't be a political issue, and yet for thirty years, the pro-gun/anti-gun debate has been a deflection from the real issue. It's both a mental health problem *and* a gun problem, not either/or.

We first need to recognize how culture has changed in the past fifty-plus years. In some rural areas, it was once normal for kids to bring guns to school because they would be going hunting with their family afterward. But we're living in a different world now.

The mental health situation in the US has been on a steady decline, so who has guns matters. We're failing our communities because we are not amending laws and improving background checks. Guns keep falling into the hands of the wrong people because of these failures.

Individuals must also be more diligent, especially family members. We have too many instances where someone has made a threat—even been arrested—and then a family member goes out and gives them a gun. They enable poor choices instead of holding their family member accountable and getting them the help they truly need.

As I was working on this book, the mother of the Oxford shooter was found guilty of involuntary manslaughter.[11] In the investigation of the 2021 shooting in which four students were killed, it was found she helped supply him with a gun, despite knowing he was struggling with suicidal ideation and warning signs which had also been dismissed by school officials.

Whether you're pro-Second Amendment or anti-gun, we all need to wake up to the fact that arguing over guns is a deflection from the real issue. By all means, we need better mental health care support. But we should also pass new laws and create better systems. At the

---

11   Elise Hammond and Tori Powell, "Mother of Oxford, Michigan, School Shooter Found Guilty of Manslaughter," CNN, February 6, 2024, accessed February 13, 2024, https://www.cnn.com/us/live-news/oxford-shooting-jennifer-crumbley-trial-verdict/index.html.

time of writing, twenty-two states have passed red flag laws which authorize the temporary seizure of firearms from an individual when it's deemed they are a danger to themselves or others.[12] If Tennessee had one of these laws in place, it could have helped prevent the Covenant Presbyterian shooter from getting a weapon.

But let's be honest—no law or system is perfect. Unsafe people will always manage to find ways to get a gun, including stealing them as we've seen in multiple cases.

Which means the best way we can take control is through the measures we put in place for protection. We can make this happen through preparation and training, effective lockdown systems, improved threat reporting, and faster police response. If an active shooter keeps failing to kill because they encounter the barriers you set up, that's how you win. That's how you stay one step ahead and end the story of an active shooter.

Instead, let's shift our focus to what's proven to help:

- Protecting kids from bullying.
- Providing the right physical security measures (locks, doors, lockdown systems).
- Preparing staff with lifesaving training (including how to stop blood loss from a bullet wound).
- Preventative actions, like better reporting of threats made online.

It's on these specific, actionable items where we will focus the next several chapters. We'll go further into detail on what actions need to be taken before an active shooter situation, what should be done during one, and what to do afterward.

---

12   World Population Review, "Red Flag Law States 2024," WorldPopulationReview. com, accessed April 4, 2024, https://worldpopulationreview.com/state-rankings/ red-flag-laws-states.

CONCLUSION

Ever since Sandy Hook, it's been clear to me that if we start training all our school staff the right way and equipping them on how to survive and stop an active shooter, we could make a difference. We need good, proven training coupled with products that actually work to slow down an attacker while speeding up police response. We need technology and systems that notify everyone in the school they are under attack—including parents. The same technology needs to notify police and first responders to get to the scene to stop the attacker.

No one single solution exists. Each plan and product must be tailored to the school. Everything needs to work together to get the best outcome—stopping the attacker in their tracks.

The final myth I've had to face was believing Sandy Hook would get us all on the same page. The fight has been more difficult than I ever imagined. You likely have the same frustrations, or you wouldn't have picked up this book. Why can't politicians see that we need minimum standards for security and funding nationwide to implement real protection in our schools? If we can send $100 billion of aid to help foreign nations at war, why can't we prioritize ending the war in our schools?

Recently, the government passed a bill for *seven-hundred billion dollars*, primarily to hire eighty-seven thousand armed IRS federal agents. This makes no sense. Why aren't we funding federal agents to protect our *schools* and put them in place like we did by implementing air marshals on domestic flights after 9/11?

I'm not naive enough to believe we will ever all agree on every issue. But we ought to agree on *this* issue. In the meantime, let's do what we can with what we have to save lives. Let's do everything we can to at least *be prepared*.

|3|

BE PREPARED

In the wake of Uvalde, I was on a Zoom call with a school district located outside of Dallas, Texas, when the administrators told me they wanted Level 1 bullet-resistant glass on their main entries only.

Perplexed by this, I asked, "Why do you want Level 1 glass when it only stops three rounds from a 9 mm handgun but zero rounds from an AR15? And why only the front door when the attackers in Uvalde and Parkland both entered through back doors?"

The head of security gave me an answer I wasn't expecting: "Look, we need to shut up the parents who are complaining we need to do something in response to Uvalde. Even if it is Level 1 bullet-resistant glass, they will think it's bullet-proof, and that is better than nothing."

Since my camera was on, I'm sure they saw my jaw drop. When I finally found my words, I said, "I don't think we are the right company for your project."

At Armoured One, we strive to do every job right and with integrity. If they weren't willing to take the correct steps to be prepared—if they were willing to mislead parents into a false sense of security—then I was happy to walk away from the situation. No job or amount of money is worth taking when there could be blood on our hands for taking actions we *know* are not right.

We tell people all the time that a false sense of security is worse than no security at all. When you believe that you can just sit there and wait for someone to rescue you—or for a product to save you—then you are waiting to meet death. The bottom line is that having a false sense of security makes people more vulnerable.

Instead of silencing parents, you have to fight for the lives of everyone in your school. Take every precaution to protect *everyone* in your school.

As mentioned, it's often a matter of wrong priorities. A school district will pass a bond for an NFL-level football field, yet they want to cut corners on safety equipment and training. Some of these schools will spend $50 million on a stadium but can't spend $250,000 on classroom door locks. They would rather keep their existing door handles which need to be locked from the hallway—meaning their staff would have to put themselves into danger's way.

I'm not afraid of confrontation, so I've asked schools about this—how they can justify spending millions on sports but not thousands on better security measures. Often, the responses I get come straight from the myths we covered: "It won't happen here."

Let's not kid ourselves. None of us know the future. You could be in a car wreck today by no fault of your own. Don't you want to make sure the seat belt is working?

Putting on a seat belt is inconvenient. It's uncomfortable. At least, that's what I heard over and over back when I wrote tickets to drivers who I caught without seat belts on. Whenever they objected to the inconvenience, I'd remind them of the inconvenience of cleaning up a fatal wreck. I'd seen too many people die in accidents because they didn't have a seat belt on.

Convenience must come second to safety. One rule I teach every school we work with: If it's convenient for you, it's convenient for a shooter. The point is to put systems in place which make an attack incredibly inconvenient for them to carry out.

For the rest of this chapter, we're going to focus on how to be prepared—how to put the "seat belt" on your school. Whether you're in school leadership or in law enforcement, you need to know what's *not* working—and what *is* working.

My philosophy is pretty simple: You have to think like a shooter. In anti-terrorism courses, you have to actually play the role of an attacker. The instructor will ask, "How would you go in there to inflict maximum casualties? What's your plan of attack?"

It sounds grim—because it is. But it's necessary to think this way to find the gaps in your security.

With this in mind, I'm not going to mention many specific tools or product names here. We want to keep our exact strategy close to the chest so a potential shooter doesn't know the plan. Because once they do, they gain an advantage. But the specific recommendations we make are based on an individual location's needs—there's no one-size-fits-all solution.

So, the advice here sticks to more generic actions which you can then apply to your community's situation. As always, I advocate for everyone to have a certified security expert's guidance on specific actions to take.

SCHOOL POLICIES AND PROTOCOLS

Many of the recurring problems we see come down to bad policies and bad training in schools. Often this is because they didn't have a knowledgeable expert to guide them in what protocols actually work in active shooter situations.

RUN, HIDE, AND FIGHT

As I've mentioned before, "Run, Hide, and Fight" has been a proven strategy for active shooter situations. Yet, many schools take issue with the word "fight" and throw out the entire strategy. Or else, they try to rebrand it. I've seen schools adapt the language to "Avoid, Deny, Defend" and "Avoid, Barricade, and Confront"—all because they want to avoid using *fight*.

We have to think of the word *fight* here not in the sense of an MMA-style smackdown but in the same way we would say "fight for your life." It's not about picking a fight with the shooter—it's about saving lives. No one is offended when we say to fight cancer, diabetes, or heart disease, so we should look at the word "fight" in the same way.

You might wonder what the problem is with changing the name of the strategy if it teaches the same tactics. The problem is that these other wordings are more difficult to understand. If you hire a new staff member from another district where they had "Avoid, Deny, Defend" but you call it "Avoid, Barricade, Confront," then it creates confusion.

If we're going to keep people safe, we need to speak the same language across the country. By reducing confusion, we increase safety for everyone. If "Run, Hide, Fight" is good enough to be the official stance for both Homeland Security and the FBI, then it should be for every school across the nation.

FIGHTING BACK

Unfortunately, many schools actually discourage teachers from protecting students by making official policies that if a teacher fights back against a *student* attacker, then they will be fired for doing so—even when the student is actively seeking to kill and injure others. In essence, they're saying, "Thanks for your courage and saving the lives of children, but you can't work here anymore." It's absurd.

It's one thing for a staff member to strike a child who is only misbehaving in a class. That's abuse and should be dealt with immediately and with zero tolerance. It's an entirely different matter when that student is hauling around an AR15 and walks into a classroom ready to kill.

Sometimes, you'll hear of cases where a staff confronted a student and de-escalated them, even getting them to hand over their weapons. But these are isolated incidents. More often than not, this doesn't work out, and the teacher is shot, leaving their students undefended.

Therefore, we do not recommend trying to talk a shooter down because they are there to kill. We saw this happen in the 2024 Perry High School shooting in Iowa when Principal Dan Marburger attempted to talk down the shooter and was killed. He was a hero for putting himself between the shooter and innocent students.[13]

On September 20, 2017, a teacher in Illinois, Angela McQueen, saw a freshman student pull out a gun and begin to fire it at students, so she sprang into action. She had always taken active shooter training seriously, and her actions saved lives that day. She was able to detain the shooter and force his gun to face the ceiling until the SRO disarmed him and arrested him. Only one student was injured because of her quick action.[14] She is a hero, period.

You have to ask yourself, if it was your loved one in that classroom, wouldn't you want the teacher to do everything in their power to save your loved one's life? Of course you would.

---

13   Khaleda Rahman, "Iowa Principal Dies Protecting Students in School Shooting," MSN.com, January 15, 2024, https://www.msn.com/en-us/news/other/iowa-principal-dies-protecting-students-in-school-shooting/ar-AA1mZv2S.

14   Associated Press, "Teacher Who Stopped Shooter Speaks about Her Experience," *State Journal-Register*, updated December 1, 2017, accessed April 4, 2024, https://www.sj-r.com/story/news/2017/12/01/teacher-who-stopped-shooter-speaks/16926927007/.

By the way, if you're a teacher reading this and you ever find yourself in such a situation where you're let go over protecting students from an attacker, Armoured One will gladly find a place for you on our team. Just reach out.

BARRICADING AND EVACUATION

Likewise, we've seen schools which also have policies against barricading and evacuation in active shooter events. Let's start with barricading.

Armoured One's sister company—ONE Training—conducts staff training for active shooter response. In our training, we teach "Run, Hide, Fight," but with one tweak—we teach "Run, Hide, *Barricade*, Fight." What we're communicating is that once you are hidden, you should do anything you can to slow down an attacker from getting into the room. Block the door with a bookshelf, desk, chairs—whatever you have on hand.

In Uvalde, this was one of their policies in place because Chief Arredondo had recommended it. After the shooting, the school changed this policy because they saw how barricading could have saved lives that terrible day.

The primary resistance to barricades comes from school staff and firefighters who express concerns about the risk of a fire breaking out. However, statistically speaking, this is not accurate. Most schools are constructed with fire-resistant materials that can withstand forty-five to ninety minutes of fire exposure. This means that walls, ceiling tiles, glass, tables, chairs, and other materials can endure at least forty-five minutes of fire before being compromised.

It's also important to note that no student has lost their life in a K–12 school due to a fire in the past forty years. It comes down to common sense—if you were able to move something in front of the door to barricade, then you can move it out of the way if you need to.

In the tragic incident at Columbine High School in 1999, the two attackers had close to a hundred bombs, detonating over forty. Despite this, not a single firefighter entered the school for over four hours, and there were no fatalities caused by fire or smoke inhalation. Some of the bombs were similar to propane tanks used for barbecue grills, but these explosive devices were contained within the school building and were self-extinguished due to the school's fire-retardant construction.

Of all the school shootings that have happened over the years, not one child has died from a fire. They've died for one reason: because the shooter was able to reach them.

Some schools also have policies against evacuation during active shooter events. They tell staff that students have to stay put—even if there is a way for them to run out of the building to safety. The fear is that a child will get lost while running away from a building.

This is inconsistent with how many schools conduct fire drills, though, where they teach staff and students to evacuate to outside the school. Also, no child has ever been lost by evacuating from an active shooter situation. In the Sandy Hook shooting, several children ran for their lives during the event. They were found several hours later, playing hopscotch and being kept safe in a local's driveway. And keep in mind it was the middle of December in Connecticut, and yet, they didn't freeze to death either.

While the fears of fire and a child being lost are well-intentioned, these policies have the potential to increase danger rather than reduce it.

911 AND LOCKDOWN AUTHORIZATION

Some school districts restrict authorization for who is allowed to call 911 and issue a lockdown order. These schools have policies which require staff to first call the main office to communicate an active shooter situation, and then someone at the main office is responsible for calling 911. Such a bad policy delays everything—especially police action.

Likewise with lockdown authorization. There are schools that limit the number of people who can issue a lockdown order, but if safety is the priority, then you should allow any staff member to issue the order. You never know where an attacker could come from.

Coach Silva and her class of third grade students were at the outdoor gymnasium of Robb Elementary when the Uvalde attacker crashed his grandfather's truck into the ravine a couple of hundred yards away. She heard the crash and made her way to see what was happening. In less than a minute, she was back on the playground, heard gunshots, and then saw a man dressed in black with a gun and bag jump over the school fence.

She had a two-way radio and used it to call for help and to warn everyone about what she had seen and heard—while simultaneously moving the kids to safety inside. As she hustled the third graders into one of the buildings, the attacker shot at her and her students. During this time, she radioed again to report the attacker was now shooting at them. It was 11:29 a.m., and lockdown should have been called by the office staff responsible with manning the radio.

Though Coach Silva was able to get the students inside and barricade them in a room, no one in the main office heard her calls for help. They did not call 911 or lockdown the school for another three minutes. Those few minutes could have changed everything. Instead, the teachers and students in rooms 111 and 112 continued to watch *Lilo and Stitch* in their classroom instead of preparing to run, hide, barricade, or fight for their lives.

Coach Silva is a hero—she not only saved her students but attempted to let everyone know the school was under attack even as she was being shot at herself. But the sad fact remains—had the lockdown been issued sooner, the story could have been different.

This is beginning to change some with new measures like Alyssa's Law in Florida, Texas, and New York. This law requires school districts to have silent panic buttons installed in every classroom so that any teacher can easily press it.

There is still some limitation here because when you press such a panic button, it doesn't tell 911 whether you're pressing it because a child is choking or because of a fire or an active shooter, so it's essential any teacher to also be able to call and provide details about the emergency. Schools with these restrictive policies should ask themselves why they trust their staff to be in charge of twenty-plus children in a classroom, but they don't trust them to push a button for an emergency.

Allowing all members of school staff to press a lockdown button would be a major step forward in getting automated alerts out and automatic doors locked within seconds. Beyond lockdown buttons, teachers should automatically have the authority to use the PA system and radios to issue school-wide alerts.

UNDERSTAND STATIC EVENT VERSUS DYNAMIC EVENT

We often see inconsistent language being used within schools when they discuss emergency protocols. For instance, there is confusion over what qualifies as a static event versus a dynamic event. So, let's clear it up here:

Static Event—events where there is no immediate threat of danger to one's life.

Dynamic Event—events where there *is* an immediate threat of danger to one's life.

For instance, an ice storm warning would be static. The school may choose to close early to allow parents to pick up students before the storm hits. But a tornado warning where there is an active storm headed toward the school would be dynamic. A stolen iPhone would be a static event while a gas leak would be dynamic.

Where this gets more difficult to decipher is with incidents where there has been abuse. For example, let's say a student comes to you and reports they were molested by their uncle four months ago. Obviously, this is terrible and needs to be reported, but it qualifies as a static event because it happened in the past. Meanwhile, a student sexually assaulting another student in a locker room would be a dynamic event.

Hearing gunshots, seeing an armed assailant, or even a bomb threat should all be treated as dynamic events requiring immediate action. Which brings us to our next point of discussion.

SCHOOL TRAINING AND RESPONSE

Next, we need to look at how schools conduct training for active shooter response. We often find inconsistencies, poor practices, and lack of preparation in cases—all of which led to lost lives. To address this, we have two recommendations:

- Use proven training.

- Standardize your response protocols.

Too often, schools default to using whatever training is free. The real question is how do you know which training is proven? It's easy for someone to come in and present themselves as an expert. For our part, we never mind some skepticism and questions from school leadership about the training we do at ONE Training. It's always recommended to ask questions and know what you're getting.

USE PROVEN TRAINING

If the training you're using isn't incorporating strategies based on proven tactics, then it may not be worth anything. As mentioned before, many schools assume they can get training from their local law enforcement, but without mandated standards, there's no guarantee your local police have been tactically trained for active shooter scenarios. For instance:

- Is your police department adequately staffed to provide training for all employees? Many of them may be trained themselves, but that doesn't mean they are certified to train *others* correctly.

- Do they teach this training daily, annually, or every five years?

- How much are you actually saving from the "free" training by your local police when you consider the overtime cost for the police *and* the staff? Could it be more financially prudent to hire a professional training company that specializes in daily training?

You should always be asking these questions whenever considering someone to train your staff.

Proven training begins with the trainer themselves. Do they have the know-how? Have they been certified? A baggage handler at an airport is an expert at handling baggage, not flying the plane. The reverse is true—a pilot shouldn't be telling a baggage handler how to do *their* job. They have vastly different skills even though they are both working in the airline industry.

Likewise, there are many FBI agents out there who are not field workers but have desk jobs—they don't know how to chase down a fugitive. A corrections officer is an expert on prison—their job is to keep people inside. That doesn't make them an expert on keeping people *out*.

Yet, we keep seeing schools trained by local law enforcement because it's free, but they haven't done the due diligence to see if proven tactics are being used. An officer may be response trained without being an expert in active shooter security measures.

Sometimes, schools bring in the wrong type of experts to consult on their security needs. For instance, I saw a city school in New York that hired a self-proclaimed expert to do their training. This individual had written multiple books about active shooters, but they were not qualified or experienced to teach on response. They might be a great researcher and writer, but when lives are on the line, you need someone who is certified. This particular individual lacks a background in law enforcement or the military and has never been involved in a critical dynamic incident. Asserting expertise in a field where one holds no relevant experience is insane. It's akin to a police officer entering an operating room and offering to perform tonsil surgery on your child just because they read about the procedure.

I've also seen schools that will bring in parents who have lost children in other school shootings and have them train their staff and consult on their security needs. But just because someone has lost a child in a terrible tragedy doesn't make them an expert on proper security. I lost my forty-year-old brother to a heart attack, but this doesn't make me qualified to do heart surgery.

Schools often listen to their ideas because of the emotional appeal. I get it. My heart breaks for them, too. Nor am I denying these individuals have helpful experience to share. Many of them are experts on dealing with terrible loss. They've seen the inaction and gaps in the system, and they're trying to do something about it. But many of them are only able to speak from their own experience, and their recommendations aren't backed up by proof.

Making recommendations that could get someone else's child killed is dangerous.

An exception to this is Michele Gay, who lost her daughter at Sandy Hook. She started up Safe and Sound Schools and has done an excellent job of becoming an expert on security by learning from true experts in law enforcement. Instead of assuming her ideas were the best, she talked with others and found best practices and is now using her platform to make schools safer.

Schools can determine if a training is proven by simply asking questions before they bring someone in. What is their training based on? What is their experience with school security? Have they been certified? If the trainer is only basing their "training" on their own ideas, then it's not proven.

Instead, whoever is conducting a training should be a true subject matter expert. A good litmus test here is whether the person is someone a judge would call upon as a witness in court to speak on a piece of evidence.

This is exactly what we saw go wrong in Uvalde. Chief Arredondo lacked expertise in active shooter training and had no real idea of what physical security needed to be in place. During our investigation, we discovered that of the eight Uvalde campuses, not a single one had a designated secure area. This was a major oversight in their training which would have been addressed by a certified trainer.

Would you hire a principal who has never worked in a school before? Would you hire a football coach who can't name all the positions? Would you hire an art teacher who has only visited museums but never studied art? Of course not. You consider people's credentials, their skills, their work history, and then you interview them.

Why would you *not* do the same for something as important as your safety?

TRAINING STUDENTS

As a company, it's our policy to *not* train students, even though this has cost us opportunities. Some schools are adamant they want their students trained exactly the same way their staff are trained. We feel deeply this is not the right approach.

When it comes to training students, the primary focus should be on awareness based on what's age appropriate. It's essential we do not cause undue trauma where they are afraid to go to school. For starters, children in grades K–5 should have a different discussion than children grades 6–8 or grades 9–12. With children in sixth grade and up, there should be discussions about suicide—how to recognize the symptoms and what to do if a friend is talking about suicide, including how to call the Suicide Hotline.

Reinforce gun safety with children by teaching students not to touch a gun if they see one and to report it to an adult. We need to reinforce with parents the importance of keeping weapons locked and out of reach of children. One shooter knew his friend's family kept a gun under their couch, stole it, and used it in his attack. The Sandy Hook shooter had access to his weapons because they belonged to his mother, whom he also killed.

We need to teach children to take threats seriously. If their friend is showing aggression and makes a threat, they need to know how to report it by telling their parents and calling 911. Too many times, we've heard the same story from friends and acquaintances of shooters: "We didn't think they were serious. We thought they were just blowing off steam."

These are all great ways to train children in safety. But there's a deeper reason why we don't teach children the same protocols and procedures that we teach to staff members: Nearly 80 percent of the time, the shooter is a former or current student.[15] It would be like showing your playbook to the opposing team.

In Uvalde, the shooter targeted classrooms 111 and 112—the rooms where he himself had been a fourth-grade student. None of us want to believe one of our students would resort to such heinous actions, but time after time, this is the trend we see—former and current students as the attackers.

This doesn't mean you can't still safely train children without the trauma of calling it "an active shooter drill." Simply call it a "lockdown drill" since it's still an accurate, simple description. Training children should be focused on teaching them to follow instructions, no matter what the emergency is. It should be done with great kindness and without fear.

So, if your school has been doing active assailant drills—STOP! Make it abundantly clear with children you're only doing a drill. Send out mass notifications to parents to let them know a lockdown drill is being performed that day and there is no real danger.

We've seen schools that tried to simulate lockdown drills without making it clear it's a drill. Next thing you know, kids are calling and texting their parents that there's a shooter—and then parents get into a wreck rushing to the school. As I write, there's an active lawsuit in Florida over this issue—a school did a so-called "drill" by having police storm in with guns drawn to simulate a real event, leaving students traumatized.

One elementary school in New York had an awful experience when they hired a self-proclaimed active shooter expert to train their

---

15 Amy Rock, "K-12 School Shooting Statistics: 52 Years of Data," Campus Safety Magazine, October 5, 2023, accessed April 9, 2024, https://www.campussafety-magazine.com/safety/k-12-school-shooting-statistics-everyone-should-know/.

students and staff. She went around, beating on doors, yelling, "Let me in!" and terrifying both staff and students alike.

When it comes to training children, follow the two Cs: *Calm* and *Communication*.

One of the best programs I've seen for training children comes from retired marine Jake Edwards who fought at Fallujah. When he teaches children, he focuses on awareness and quick response, using kid-friendly language.

For instance, he doesn't talk directly about shooters. He says, "What if a shark could come up on land? How would you get away from it?" He uses this to teach them situational awareness and how to find the quickest routes to safety. What's great about this training is it's not just for active shooter scenarios but can also apply to fires and inclement weather. He gives kids just enough info to keep them safe without traumatizing them.

Some schools will train kids to sit crisscross on their bottoms during drills. But this makes it more difficult to flee if they needed to. So, what Jake does is teach kids to take a knee so they can pop up faster if they end up needing to run for their lives: "If that shark is coming toward you, you can get up a lot faster from the knee position than sitting crisscross."

STANDARDIZE RESPONSE PROTOCOLS

One of the groups I recommend is the I Love U Guys Foundation. The founders—Ellen and John-Michael Keyes—lost their daughter in the Platte Canyon shooting in 2006. During the shooting, their daughter Emily sent each of them the same text message: "I love u guys." Those would be her last recorded words.

From this tragedy, I Love U Guys has done an incredible job of engaging communities and stressing the importance of consistent, proven response training in schools. One of the tactics they teach is for K–12 schools to use standardized response language.

For instance, Texas has over 1,200 school districts, representing over 9,000 campuses. Yet, districts and campuses often use their own coding system for emergencies—some will say "code red," others "code brown" for the same type of event. When staff change districts, they have to learn a whole new set of codes, which can lead to confusion and mistakes.

One note of special importance is that codes should only be used in a *static* event so you're not causing alarm. When I was a cop, we had a code specifically for when we were going to make an arrest but didn't want to aggravate the individual we're about to handcuff—especially since that would make our job more difficult. But if the suspect became violent and pulled out a gun, the time for codes was gone. We wouldn't shout, "Code X"; we'd use clear language: "He's got a gun!"

Likewise, once an event becomes dynamic, use plain language. There's nothing wrong with having codes, but make them consistent and only use them in static events. For instance, I Love U Guys teaches five standard crisis responses:

██

This is used when hallways need to be kept clear and is always followed up by the directive, "In your room or area."

██

Used to safeguard people inside a building, followed with the directive, "Get inside. Lock outside doors." Ideally, your external doors will always be locked, but more on this later.

██

Used when you need to secure individual rooms and keep everyone in place and quiet. This should be the protocol for active shooter situations, followed up with the directive, "Locks, lights, out of sight." In other words, lock the door to the room, turn the light off (or obstruct the window), and hide. You want to do anything you can to get out of a shooter's line of sight.

█████████

Use this when you need to move people from one location to another, whether that's inside or outside of the building. Be ready to follow it up with more directions. However, in an active shooter situation, you want to be cautious to avoid telling the shooter where you're headed when doing this over a PA or radio.

██████

When this protocol is issued, it should be accompanied with a statement about the exact hazard and safety strategy to use for group and self-protection. For instance, "Shelter. Tornado Warning. Move away from external walls and windows."[16]

Let's hone in on "lockdown" for a moment. Any time the term is used, it should mean one thing—someone is there to kill or hurt. In New York schools, I saw a bad practice where they used two different terms in their procedures—*lockdown* and *lockout*. They had both of these terms in their official materials they sent out to everyone in the district.

When I brought this problem to the state officials' attention, they said it would cost too much to reprint and resend the info. They told me, "Everyone here knows the difference."

We started advocating for them to change the language in 2012, and it was finally implemented in 2024. It took twelve years for state

---

16   Adapted from content on ILoveUGuys.org, "Standard Response Protocol," accessed on February 15, 2024, https://iloveuguys.org/The-Standard-Response-Protocol.html.

officials to recognize the potential danger to lives because of the similarities between "lockdown" and "lockout."

Never assume people "know the difference," especially if you consider that whenever someone is panicked and it's a high-risk situation, it's already easy to misunderstand these terms when they get called out. They're too similar in sound.

On that note, schools need to make sure there is enough differentiation in signals. Uvalde sits near the border, so they consistently get alerts related to illegal immigration issues. Their alert system in the school would sound a tone designated for them to go into a hold. In 2022, this alert had been issued *forty-five times* from February through May. It had practically become white noise.

Unfortunately, it's the same tone the school's PA system used for the lockdown alert. So, even though the lockdown alert was issued at 11:32 a.m., it caused confusion for the staff because it wasn't clear it was a lockdown alert versus a hold alert. As a result, many classrooms did nothing different—such as the class that continued to watch a movie as the shooter made his way throughout the school.

Failure to communicate clearly costs lives, as it did in Parkland. The morning of the attack, the school did a fire drill, and they told staff to leave everything behind and lock their doors. This was the official policy because they were concerned about theft. On the third floor of Building 12, when the alarm sounded, teachers repeated the fire drill protocols and went out into the halls, locking their doors behind them. When the shooter entered the hallway, they were fully exposed and couldn't get back into their rooms quickly.

As noted above, there's no need for staff and students to be trained *exactly* the same. Students won't be hitting any lockdown buttons or issuing alerts—just following staff directions. We recommend staff training take place on a staff development day when students are not around. Take the morning to run through everything with a certified trainer and give space for questions so everyone can be crystal clear on their responsibilities.

Finally, as we transition to law enforcement, every school should standardize how they interact with police. You need standard protocols and training on how to admit police into the building. We see schools that only designate one person in the front office as the liaison responsible for handing over a key to let law enforcement in. Instead, you should make sure every staff member has the ability to hand over a key. Remember—you never know which side of the campus a shooter may come from.

In smaller communities, you may even consider letting police have a set of keys or electronic-controlled access card/fob at whatever station is closest to a campus. Even so, you still need to make sure you have protocols for staff admitting police in the event the responding officers don't have the keys on hand. After all, it's better for them to head straight to the school than have to go to the station first to pick up a set of keys.

Additionally, create maps of the campus layout—both paper and digital copies they can easily access. Include clear, standardized room and building numbers. We'll talk about signage more in the next chapter, but keep in mind that not all of the officers will know the layout of the school. They won't know where "the art room" is or which room is "Mr. Graham's classroom."

Since many schools don't have SROs, it becomes even more important for law enforcement to have maps on hand. At least once a year, invite local law enforcement to walk through your campuses and learn the layout of the land. This will help them better understand how to move through the school if they ever need to respond. Because even if you do have an SRO on staff, what happens if they are injured or killed while confronting a shooter? The police who arrive on the scene will need to know where to go without delay.

LAW ENFORCEMENT POLICIES, PROTOCOLS, AND TRAINING

As we've already touched on several times, police response is a major factor in staying one step ahead of an active shooter. The faster they can get to the shooter, the more lives that can be saved. Through all of our investigations, we've seen various trends which separate the good policies and protocols from the bad.

IMMEDIATE ACTION, NOT DISCRETIONARY ACTION

We find too many police departments that have policies about waiting until a certain number of police arrive before going into an active shooter situation. Often, this means it's left up to the discretion of the officers on-site to decide when to take action. Instead, the universal policy for K–12 responses should be an immediate willingness to go in and lay down your life, whether you have backup or not.

The day after the shooting in Uvalde, I found an officer who had been inside the building during the attack. At first, he was very limited on what he would tell me—only that Chief Arredondo had been in charge and had felt that the scene went from a dynamic event to a static event.

In response, I told the officer, "An active shooter does not get to decide to be inactive. It is an active shooter until he is arrested or neutralized."

The officer dropped his head and said, "I agree." He started crying and said, "I let my community down, and I should have told the chief that his orders to wait were wrong. I wish I died yesterday instead of those kids."

It was crushing to hear this. As he had been trained to do, he was obeying orders from a chief but fully regretted it. With my tactical background in SWAT, it was clear to me the chief was clueless on how to respond to a dynamic event.

I know for a fact that all of the SWAT operators I served with in New York would have run into that school immediately. We didn't come from a huge agency, but I served with some amazing men and women whose goal was to protect lives at all costs.

Whether it was arrogance or ignorance, Chief Arredondo should have handed over command to someone with more tactical experience. Being a great leader does not mean you are always in charge of the decision. It means you surround yourself with great people who have expertise in different fields. Just because you hold a higher rank than someone else doesn't mean you have all the answers.

Meanwhile, during the Covenant Presbyterian shooting in Nashville, Officer Rex Engelbert arrived on scene and immediately took action. He instantly got out of his patrol vehicle, listened to directions from a teacher who held out the key so he could get into the building, and went in to confront and neutralize the attacker. He responded like a SWAT operator and didn't hesitate to take action, despite the danger to himself.

In many rural communities, it could take at least fifteen minutes for an officer to reach a school—there's no time to waste. Otherwise, you end up with lawsuits like what happened in Parkland because the SRO wouldn't go in. He defended his lack of response based on there being too much discretion in the rules from the sheriff's office, which was where he'd been trained.

All too often, discretionary action policies have led to fatal mistakes. Policies requiring immediate action consistently save lives.

TRAIN TO PROTECT

It's alarming how few police departments make it a priority to train for active shooter situations. In my opinion, if you have both a badge and gun in your role, then you should be trained for active shooter response the same way you are for any other part of your job. You never know when you'll need those tactical skills.

Ideally, training for active shooter response should be state-mandated law. Until it is, though, police departments need to take it upon themselves to make this an office mandate and conduct training on at least an annual basis, just like other yearly training requirements. These are hands-on trainings—not digital courses or videos—where you are put into a simulated environment.

All too often, I see training not being taken seriously in police departments. Many states have policies where police have to get an 80 percent accuracy rating at a shooting range, yet I've seen cases of police supervisors just signing themselves off instead of actually doing it. They believe they are "above the law" in this sense, that it's not worth their time.

Part of why Officer Engelbert and his backup, Officer Collazo, responded so well in Nashville is because of how seriously they take training. Chief Drake of the Nashville PD requires all his staff— around 1,500 cops—to go through active shooter training every year. They utilize an abandoned mall for their active shooter training, using simunition guns (kind of like paintball guns) so they can make it as real as possible. This comes out to a lot of overtime, but they know it saves lives. They've trained over a decade for those four minutes of response at Covenant Presbyterian.

The numbers sadly tell the difference in training readiness: twenty-one killed in Uvalde compared with six in Nashville.

If you're not willing to train to protect, then get another job. One where you don't have to lay down your life for people. Otherwise, you end up with a Uvalde-type situation where cops were restraining parents who wanted to run into the school to save their kids—when those cops should have been running in.

BUILDING SECURITY MEASURES

More times than I can count, I've had SROs admit to me, "I don't know what to do if a shooter were to come in. Can you explain to me how glass security works? What should we actually be doing? What kind of locks should we be using?"

And too often, these SROs go back to their superintendent with our recommendations, only to be ignored. Schools keep spending millions on purely aesthetic updates, such as one school I advised that spent $80 million to make it look like Google headquarters—yet, they won't spend $100,000 on updated lockdown systems.

It's true that updating the security measures in your building can be costly. No one denies that. But it's still far less than losing even one precious child's life—and it's also less than a stack of lawsuits.

I know this can be a confusing part of the process, especially when there are companies out selling products that aren't any good. In the next chapter, I'm going to give you some guidelines you can use to know the products that work from the shoddy ones that will fail. But for now, we'll focus on some best practices for how to update your building security.

One which should be a minimum standard is to install exterior doors which automatically stay *locked*. In other words, they can only be opened with a key—whether a physical key or electronic access key. This type of lock is called a storeroom lock.

Often, what I hear from schools is they don't like these doors because it's inconvenient to always have to unlock them to get in. But remember: *If it's convenient for you, it's convenient for a shooter.* And this was one of the biggest security failures in Uvalde—the back door closed but did not automatically lock, and the shooter was able to walk right in.

If you're able to spring for it, electronic access doors which require a keycard are a good balance of secure and convenient. Even better, install electronic access control systems where staff can use an app on their smartphones to unlock doors. This is even more secure than a keycard since keycards can be dropped and used by a shooter. Since most smartphones now use security measures like a passcode or Face ID to unlock, it adds another barrier of entry for an attacker. Plus, keycards get lost every day—not many people lose or lend out their cell phones!

Regarding doors, you need to make sure interior doors (classroom doors) can be locked from the *inside* of the room. Many schools have classroom doors which can only be locked from the outside. This means a teacher would have to open the door and go into the hallway to lock it, possibly exposing themselves to the attacker.

As I mentioned before, the alarm button used in Uvalde wasn't a true lockdown button, leading to confusion over the nature of the emergency being signaled. A true, high-security lockdown button would automatically do the following:

- Close and lock any open hallway doors to restrict the shooter's movement.

- Send an emergency alert to the police.

- Shut down all school networked computers and devices with a message stating the school is in lockdown.

- Send automated messages to social media accounts and text messages to alert parents that the school is in lockdown and that law enforcement has been contacted.

- Advise the parents in the automated message not to respond to the school so that first responders are given the opportunity to get there quickly.

- Initiate a pre-recorded voice message to go over the PA system that the school is in lockdown.

- Release and close all magnetically held open doors, which should be pre-locked. Also, it should immediately lock all automated door locking systems.

- If possible, it should also turn on flashing blue lockdown lights throughout the school.

With today's technology, all of this can happen within seconds of the button being pushed, speeding up police response, creating barriers to impede the shooter's access, and giving teachers time to hide kids, lock, and barricade doors.

Another standard should be upgrading door windows and adjoining windows to ASTM F3561 Shooter Attack–tested glass or film. Most parents and administrators want bullet-resistant glass because they believe it is bullet-proof. Though bullet-proof glass does not exist, Level 7 UL 972 bullet-resistant glass is made to stop five rounds from specific caliber bullets, such as those from an AR15. As I referenced in the last chapter, many schools don't know about glass grade levels, so they don't think to ask vendors.

Many school administrators and parents are advocating for the installation of bullet-resistant glass in all school windows. Apart from being pricey, this specialized glass is also thick and heavy, necessitating the re-engineering of frames and doors to support its weight. These modifications come with significant costs.

At the time of writing this text, these windows typically cost around $250 per square foot. Therefore, we recommend putting Level 7 glass for the greeter windows in the controlled vestibule and any special needs classrooms.

Schools should proactively develop warm relationships with local law enforcement if they haven't already. Some cities and communities are hesitant to have police officers in their schools due to concerns the officers will be seen as a threat to students, rather than as protectors. The best way to develop more rapport, though, is to have police around more in non-emergency situations. Keep in mind that many cops are also parents, so they also have a vested interest in the school's safety beyond the oath they've sworn.

We often recommend schools designate a room where police officers are welcome to take a break, catch up on their paperwork at the end of their shift, get a snack, or otherwise interact with staff and students. Their mere presence at the school can be a powerful deterrent to an attack and helps them learn the layout of the school in the event they ever need to respond to a dynamic event.

And finally, on often overlooked but easily fixed security issues: *radios.* Many schools lack the proper access to radios and relay boosters which allow them to communicate information across the school and with law enforcement. Having a two-way radio in every room, regularly testing them, and having someone monitor them is an easy way to improve your communication and keep everyone safe.

Remember, that's your first job—keeping people safe and alive.

CONCLUSION

Over the years, I realized that in order to stay one step ahead of active shooters, I needed a team of people. No one person has all the knowledge, which is why you should be wary of anyone who presents themselves or their product as being the one-stop solution. It's in collective expertise and knowledge we can make a difference.

But this goes beyond having a team of experts in active shooters, Homeland Security, ballistics, and physical security. We've also added experts in school finance, government lobbyists, and government financing/grant writing and school business. That way, when we sit down with school superintendents and school business administrators to discuss these measures, we can help them find ways to make it the priority it should be. If it's "not in the budget," then let's find out why. Let's make a way together to make our budgets match our priorities. But children's safety isn't a place to cut corners.

I know this is a lot of information to take in. You might feel a little overwhelmed and not be sure where to start. That's normal. In the next chapter, you'll find our Top Ten Commandments for Preparedness. If you prioritize that list, you'll be making your school a safer facility for students and staff—by making it a more challenging target for the would-be attacker.

4

THE TEN COMMANDMENTS OF PREPARATION

I know I've already given you a lot to think about when it comes to preparation. But when it comes down to it, this is the only area where we have full control over what happens. Time after time, it's the schools that are prepared that prove to be the safest, which shouldn't be surprising. In any part of life—interviewing for a job, getting ready for a championship game, or practicing a presentation—it often comes down to how prepared you are.

One day, I got a call from Kim Ward, a superintendent at a small school district in upstate New York. They only had two buildings and around eight hundred kids total, but she was very conscious of protecting the schools following Parkland. She asked me to come and give a presentation to her school board and construction manager.

At the meeting, she clarified I was there for more than a sales pitch. "The police can't get to us faster than fifteen minutes if something happened," she said, "so we need to know how we can be prepared for the worst."

Frankly, this was a relief to hear. There were a number of items they needed to refine with their training, their procedures, and some building issues. But after only an hour, we were able to put together a list of next steps to move forward and enhance their security measures.

Later, Kim moved to a new district with about a dozen campuses, including three thousand students just at the high school. She called me up and said, "Tom, I need you to come here. This place is a mess."

Unlike our first work together, the school board pushed back on her—and me. We heard some of the usual objections: "We don't need this level of security. This is a higher-income area. We have a low crime rate. The police station is literally a mile down the road. *It won't happen here.*"

One thing to know about Kim is she's tough and ornery in the best possible way. She was steadfast against these objections, adamant they had to make changes. The board had to cave when staff pushed back to say they wouldn't stay at a school where safety wasn't a top priority.

Compared with some other schools, they didn't even need to spend a crazy amount of money—mostly it was creating new policies and procedures. One of the physical upgrades was installing lockdown buttons which would close the fire doors when punched, including hardened glass. Another one was giving the staff-controlled access keycards and fobs.

Another alteration was creating a check-in system at the front where someone would have to be vetted at a greeter window—one with bullet-resistant glass so the greeter could move to safety in time if shots were fired at the window. As part of our full security assessment, we also updated training for the staff, teaching them "Run, Hide, Fight," including the need to barricade after hiding.

Not long after all these measures were put in place, there was an incident involving one of their students. He had been expelled and, due to some mental health and substance abuse issues, had also spent some time in a psych ward. After he was released, he got high again and jumped on social media to say he was headed to the school to kill people.

He showed up at the school with a weapon and came up to the front doors. One aspect of their security where they hadn't followed our recommendation was about having the exterior front doors at the greeter vestibule locked at all times. They had pushed back on this as a matter of convenience because they didn't want to have to constantly buzz people in and were afraid it would make the school feel like a prison. Plus, given the winters, they were worried about leaving people out in the cold and wanted visitors to be able to get into the vestibule where it would be warm and dry. Since the doors from the vestibule into the school were controlled access, they felt like this was enough.

While those reasons all make sense, it's worth the reminder: *If it's convenient for you, it's convenient for a shooter.*

The other measure they weren't able to implement yet was that they couldn't afford blue lights to flash whenever the lockdown button was hit. We always suggest this measure because often, schools only have the fire alarm lights, but as we saw in Parkland, this can lead to confusion. A teacher might think it's a real fire alarm and bring their class out into a hallway, exposing them to danger—which is exactly what happened on the second floor of the Covenant Presbyterian School shooting in Nashville in 2023. With blue lights, staff know to hide and barricade immediately.

Anyway, when the student came in, the greeter recognized him as being expelled and saw his weapon. She immediately hit the lockdown button and ducked down to safety behind a brick wall, plus the bullet-resistant glass that had been installed. She yelled to the people in the offices behind her, "Lockdown, lockdown!"

The lockdown announcement played inside the school moments later, and doors were automatically locked, so he was trapped in the controlled vestibule. Inside there was an old slate desk that wasn't bolted down, used mostly for parents to drop off any items their kids may have forgotten. But once he realized the greeter window was bullet-resistant glass, he picked up the desk and started using it as a battering ram against the doors. Since these were older, aluminum-style doors, he managed to break them down after a few minutes of beating against them. Still, it slowed him down, giving more time for police response, which is exactly what you want with your security measures—*slow down the attacker.*

In fact, with the time it took him to break through the doors, many of the classrooms were actually able to evacuate and get outside of the building and hide. Those who didn't have this option had time to barricade in their classrooms and cover the door windows.

After forcing his way out of the control vestibule, the attacker found himself trapped in the atrium. No students were present in this area, only an unarmed security guard who had taken cover behind a locked pull-down gate and underneath a desk, out of sight. There was no way for him to get to any of the students that wouldn't take a ton of time and effort.

We had pushed for them to get an armed SRO, but this was another measure the school board had decided they weren't ready for—mostly because the chief of police had assured them they could be at the school within a minute if anything ever happened. Unfortunately, this was a busy day for the department—and there was no one at the police station when the 911 call came in. It would take eight minutes for them to arrive.

By the time he managed to get through the door, he was bloodied up from the glass he'd broken, which made the weapon slippery in his hands, and he dropped it. Since schools are required to have fire extinguishers, he grabbed one, attempting to break the glass in the fire doors so he could get to the students. Despite his efforts, he was unsuccessful at breaking through the glass due to the Armoured One 23-mil film treatment.

Around this time, the police arrived and confronted him with weapons drawn. He started spraying them with the fire extinguisher, but they quickly arrested him without having to fire a shot. In fact, the only person injured in the entire incident was the attacker.

When Kim called me about the incident, she was overwhelmed, almost to the point of tears. It was incredible to hear how well the staff had followed their training—they had done a phenomenal job keeping kids safe. The incident also proved where further improvements could be made—like bolting down the desk in the atrium. And needless to say, the school board quickly course-corrected and followed through on the other recommended measures, like updating the atrium doors and locking the front doors where people would have to be buzzed in from the outside.

On a Zoom call afterward, one of the school board members said, "You know, we've got media showing up to ask us what happened, and we should go out and tell them everything we did and how it all worked."

For a moment, I was selfishly tempted to say, "Yeah, sounds great." After all, it would be free advertising for the business. But after a couple seconds, I said, "Absolutely not." And his jaw dropped.

I explained, "If we do that, all we're doing is telling the next attacker what to do instead. So, I don't want our name mentioned, and you shouldn't mention the exact products used either."

Confused, he asked, "Then what's the narrative? What do we tell people when they ask what worked?"

I said, "You tell them that due to your security measures and training, he couldn't get to students—and that's why no one was killed or injured. You want the next person tempted to attack to believe this place is a fortress and not worth the risk."

Stories like this are why we do what we do—why I will continue to preach preparation to anyone who will listen. You can't control what kind of weapons an attacker shows up with—or when they show up. You can't control when the police will arrive. But you can control what you do now to discourage an attack from taking place—and if one does happen, slowing them down and keeping them away from your staff and children. It's all about staying one step ahead.

It's important to understand that it's not just about taking *any* actions but taking the *right* actions. Even though the school didn't follow all our recommendations, they followed enough of them to change the narrative. Without those measures in place, the story could've been another gruesome, tragic headline. As far as I'm concerned, Kim saved lives by being adamant about security.

When we do security assessments, it's always tailored to the individual school's needs. Kim's first school district had very different needs than the next one. There's no one-size-fits-all option, which is another reason we rarely publicize specific products. Instead, we focus on what I call the "Ten Commandments of Preparation," that is, the top ten safety recommendations for schools.

These are loosely in order of most important to least, though you should have a full security assessment to determine *your* exact needs. But if you at least follow these ten recommendations, you can save lives and help end the story of active shooter by staying one step ahead.

1. CERTIFIED ACTIVE SHOOTER TRAINING

As I've mentioned before, the training you do with your staff must follow the federal guidelines of "Run, Hide, Fight" set out by the FBI, Secret Service, and Homeland Security. This is the exact training taught by ONE Training.

In the effort to remove the word "fight," some schools have rebranded the same concept. I know a Texas school that calls it "Avoid, Deny, Defend," and another that wanted to call it "Avoid, Barricade, Confront." But these different wordings/acronyms create confusion, especially when staff move around between districts or schools. Keeping the standard, federal-level language solves this.

Also, every staff member in a school needs to be trained by a company that is certified through the NSSPA (National Safety Security Protection Association).[17] When I say every staff, I literally mean *every* staff—from the superintendent to the facilities team to substitute teachers and bus drivers. Not only does every staff member need to attend the training, but they need to be *tested* to make sure they understand their options for survival.

Many school districts balk at training these last two groups—they don't want to pay the extra money to bring substitutes and drivers in for ninety minutes to train them. But what happens if a substitute is with a class when an incident occurs?

Unfortunately, we know what can happen. At Sandy Hook, one of the victims was a substitute teacher, Lauren Rousseau (age thirty), who had dreamed of becoming a teacher ever since she had been in kindergarten. She had been hired only a month before and was substituting for a teacher who was on maternity leave when the attacker

---

17   Note: The NSSPA does not train schools themselves. Rather, it is an oversight of
      security standards for companies, products, and security recommendations.

killed her. She bravely tried to protect the children the best she knew how but wasn't properly trained.

Likewise, in the Covenant Presbyterian shooting in Nashville, substitute teacher Cindy Peak was killed during the shooting. Peak was one of three adults killed that day. The other two—Mike Hill, the assistant facilities manager, and Principal Koonce—sacrificed themselves by doing what they needed to do to keep the school safe.

The majority of US schools do not train their substitutes. But in one New Mexico school where they did require subs to be trained, a seventy-four-year-old substitute teacher, Kathleen "Katie" Potter, successfully barricaded her room with a couch and saved lives when they came under attack. Her response the day after the shooting? "If you need somebody on Monday, I'll be there."[18] I want *her* to be my kids' substitute!

Similarly, bus drivers can be a first line of defense. They should learn red flags for shooters—such as a kid who is overdressed on a warm day and carrying large duffel bags, or who has been overheard making threats. They need a protocol to follow so they don't have to pick up students they feel pose a threat—and a way to contact the school and initiate any proactive measures.

The training should not have blood or gore in it. Instead, it should be empowering—not fear-based. We recommend annual training for a minimum of ninety minutes and for districts to maintain strict documentation of who has completed their active shooter training.

I know that sounds obvious, but I've had too many conversations with heads of school security who say they're mandated to train but don't know how to prove everyone has done so. Active shooter training should be on the standard training checklist, right along with other

---

18   Amy Rock, "Substitute Teacher, Custodian Praised for Saving Lives in Aztec Shooting," Campus Safety Magazine, December 12, 2017, accessed April 17, 2024, https://www.campussafetymagazine.com/safety/staff-aztec-high-school-shooting/.

important safety trainings like reporting suspected abuse. It's not worth the lawsuit when a family comes forward after an incident to say, "My loved one wasn't trained right." Having clear documentation protects your district from having to face these kinds of litigious responses!

According to the NSSPA, the average police response time is eight minutes. If barricading makes the shooter have to fight through a door for three minutes, you increase survivability. If they manage to break through, that's when you go into "Fight" mode, doing anything you can to delay them further. If they get their arm through, by all means, staff should use what they have to injure the attacker's arm, or, if they can do so safely, disarm the attacker. But they won't know how to do this safely if they aren't trained right. More than anything else you can do, *training saves lives*. It is the *best* proven way to stay one step ahead.

2. BUILD STATE-LEVEL AND DISTRICT-LEVEL SECURITY THREAT AND BEHAVIORAL THREAT ASSESSMENT TEAMS

In many ways, this goes along with staff training. At least on the district level, you need to develop multidisciplinary and diverse assessment teams. When I say multidisciplinary and diverse, I mean that you should have people represented from across *all* areas of the school. Too often when schools develop such assessment teams, it only includes top leadership or departmental heads.

Instead, you should have representatives from not only administration and teaching but also from facilities management/custodial, food services, athletic department, extracurricular programming, and any other sectors of your school. The idea is to increase the number of trained "feet on the ground" who know what kind of threats to look for. After all, threats may be overheard by a kitchen worker or a custodian which might never be heard by a teacher.

So many shooters have been red flagged as potential attackers due to threats they've made or other indicators, but no system existed to properly communicate the signs or respond to them. Therefore, you need a team in place who can assess both verbal threats and behavioral indicators to be more proactive in response. By doing so, you may not only save the lives of children but also prevent a hurting person from ever becoming a shooter.

In the midst of a dynamic event, though, the goal for the assessment team is to *slow down* the attacker and *speed up* the police response. Anyone on the team must be trained in how to notify everyone inside and outside of the building that they are in lockdown. This includes using standardized language, as follows:

████████

Lockdown is only called when there is someone at the school trying to kill people with a gun or another deadly weapon. Staff and students should follow "Run, Hide, Barricade, Fight" depending on the situation they are in, making sure to barricade once they are in their hiding position.

Lockdown is *not* called for a fight between students or a bailout of illegal immigrants near the school. It's only for intentional or malicious acts of violence that have intent to kill.

Examples: Seeing someone with a weapon (such as a gun or knife), seeing evidence of someone who has been shot or stabbed, or hearing shots fired.

████████

Get inside the locked building and into a locked room. Make sure all exterior and interior doors are locked. Once in a locked room, it is business as usual—but keep alert for any new directives.

This should be used when events occur off school grounds but are in close proximity or could involve someone coming to the school.

Examples: A nearby bank robbery, reports of an armed suicidal person in the area, an angry parent threatening violence headed to the school, or a violent armed suspect within the school's area.

█████████

Stay in your room with the door locked and then do business as usual. We do not want movement in the hallways or outside of the school.

Examples: Medical emergencies, missing child, a fight, an angry parent in the building, and other non-life-threatening incidents.

███████

Evacuations are used to notify people to stop what they were doing and get out of the building safely. Evacuation calls should include follow-up information.

Examples: Evacuating due to a fire in the cafeteria, gas leak in the science wing, or because of a bomb threat called in.

████████

Shelter is used to notify people to get to a place of refuge, mostly for threats involving nature.

Examples: This is primarily when there is inclement weather, such as a tornado warning, hurricane warning, or a wild animal on the premises.

Threat assessments need to be completed based on the history of K–12 school shootings and active shooter events by looking at the "red flag" indicators. The data and analytics show how shooters get to their intended victims. Think of it like studying a disease. You ask: How did the person get the disease? How did it spread through the body? How did it injure or kill the patient? How was it stopped? What worked or didn't work against the disease?

We do the same for stopping active shooters. We can utilize the data and analytics from past shootings to create solutions to what went wrong by asking: How did the attacker get the weapons? How did they get into the school or room? How did they move through the building? How did they injure or kill the victims? How were they stopped? What worked or didn't work against the attacker?

The answers can lead to new solutions, including the implementation of additional safety measures, such as:

- Mental Health Awareness Training for staff

- Suicide Prevention programs for students and staff

- Anti-bullying programs

- "If You See Something, Say Something®"

- Anonymous tip lines for students or family members to call in their concerns

How many times have we all heard the comment, "He said he wanted to kill people, but we didn't think he was being serious"? Having threat assessment teams in place can keep you proactive, keep children safe, and keep your school from becoming another tragic headline.

Another task for the assessment team to carry out is to develop contingency plans. For instance, in the event of an incident, what's your plan to get children off-site once the incident is over? You may not be able to get bus drivers to the school fast enough. Or where will you move children to where they can wait for their parents off-site, so they aren't exposed to the elements?

If your town has a local metro system, have your assessment team network with them. Develop a safety plan for what it would look like to send city buses to the schools to transport children to a safe location so that law enforcement and EMS can do their jobs. Likewise, network with leaders of organizations in your area who could serve as a gathering place. Is there a local college auditorium nearby? A church with a large sanctuary? Or a government building? Any of these could be viable secondary, safe "pickup" locations.

Identify these secondary locations for each campus so that you can communicate to parents where they need to go to find their children. The last thing you want is for every parent to head to the school and clog up the roads while EMS is trying to save lives and while police are trying to begin the investigation.

3. LOCKING INTERIOR AND EXTERIOR DOORS

Over 99 percent of the time an active shooter enters the school, they enter through what the NSSPA calls a "Life Opening."[19] Over 90 percent of those times, the shooter is either let into the school or walks through an unlocked door. This is exactly what we saw with both Uvalde and Parkland—both shooters walked through unlocked exterior doors.

This is especially a shame with Parkland because it was in a wealthier school district where they could have afforded the exterior

---

19   The phrase "life opening" originally comes from law enforcement and military term "fatal funnel," referring to doorways where one can be easily seen but which are difficult to move out of in the case of incoming projectiles/bullets. The NSSPA redesignated these as "life openings," which encompasses the doorway, door, lock, door windows, sidelight, and frames.

electronic-controlled locks. At the very least, they could have had key cards, but those aren't always the best solution since they can be easily lost or lent out. Instead, they could have had electronic access on smartphones. People rarely lose their phone—and even if they do, today's phone security measures would keep a shooter from being able to access an app to unlock the door.

At the very least, all exterior doors should be locked. Yes, this means your staff will need to use a key to get in—but this slight inconvenience is worth saving lives.

Similarly, any room a student could enter should be locked during the day, *especially* while students are present. This saves teachers from having to run over to lock the door whenever a lockdown is initiated.

We recommend storeroom-style locks that cannot be put into the unlocked position. All too often, it's easy for a staff member to accidentally put regular doors into an unlocked position when they use their key.

Like Kim's school did, you should establish controlled access at all point-of-entry doorways where you want people to enter the building. While you can't always predict where a shooter will choose to enter, this is a simple adjustment for any school to make which immediately makes it more difficult for an intruder to come in, giving more time for students to get to safety and for police to arrive.

4. STANDARD RESPONSE PROTOCOL (SRP)

As addressed in the last chapter, we reference and recommend the I Love U Guys Foundation Standard Response Protocol.[20] We are working to get every school's emergency response protocol (ERP) to be standardized universally—first, statewide, and eventually, nation-

---

20   See more at https://iloveuguys.org/The-Standard-Response-Protocol.html.

wide. Students and staff should be able to move anywhere in the state and have the same exact ERP language and know what to do when a lockout is called.

Plain language should be the requirement rather than complicated codes which can be easily misunderstood or forgotten. This is exactly the confusion we witnessed at Marjory Stoneman Douglas High School in Parkland which caused some teachers thinking it was a fire emergency instead of an active shooter, leading to loss of life. Remember, in a dynamic event, emergency responders, police, and SWAT teams use plain language.

5. LOCKDOWN SYSTEM

According to the NSSPA, the average 911 call comes in to dispatch about ninety seconds after the shooting began. Before you make a call to 911, though, get yourself and any children to safety and barricade first. Only then can you safely make the call.

I can't stress this enough. We do not want someone being shot at while simultaneously taking the time to unlock their phone to call 911.

To reduce response time, every school building should have a minimum of one lockdown button (lockdown initiation) to engage a lockdown procedure. Ideally, you have multiple lockdown initiation points located throughout the school for staff access since you never know where a shooter will be coming from.

Speaking of 911, a true lockdown button will not only trigger the lockdown but will also alert 911. This is a huge positive for staying one step ahead of the shooter. However, since not everyone will have easy access to a lockdown button, they will still have to call 911 manually. But even if you have access to a lockdown button, you *should* still call 911 to provide additional details for responding officers. At the very least, though, the automated 911 alert helps cut down the response time.

Many people believe that Alyssa's Law covers a mandate for lockdown buttons in the states that have passed it, but it doesn't. What it actually mandates is a *silent panic* button/alarm in every school, which is different. Schools should take the next step to have a specific button for lockdown.

An all-purpose panic button isn't enough on its own because it doesn't tell 911 what the problem is—it could be a child having a seizure, a fire, or an active shooter. All of these require different response protocols from first responders. A lockdown button has only one meaning: "We're under attack."

To make this easier, here are the different types of emergency buttons you should know about:

PANIC BUTTON

A button that is pushed to get you help for a range of both non-life-threatening or life-threatening incidents. An example of a non-life-threatening situation would be an angry parent or a fight between students.

MEDICAL BUTTON

A button that is pushed for medical emergencies that are life-threatening like a heart attack or choking. This tells 911 to send EMT right away, not just police.

LOCKDOWN BUTTON

A button that is only pushed when an incident meets the criteria for a lockdown under the ERP. Lockdown measures are usually put into effect in response to an imminent danger to life or severe injury occurring on or near the school grounds. This would include any dynamic event such as the presence of an armed intruder, gunfire, or other critical intentional life-threatening emergencies. Pushing the lockdown button will advise staff and students to "Run, Hide, Barricade, Fight" depending on the situation they are in. Police will come to the school as fast as possible to engage the attacker.

Note that the panic, lockdown, and medical buttons should be placed at the greeter's office and then on the desks of the principal and secretary at a school. There should also be a medical button at the nurse's office. Another option is a device staff can wear around their neck called Vocera. This simply allows for them to call a lockdown, medical, or panic alert.

The following actions should happen simultaneously when the lockdown system is initiated:

- An automatic call or message goes to the 911 center letting them know that the school is in lockdown and there is someone at the building with a deadly weapon.

- A mass notification is sent out to all police, fire, and EMS stating which specific school is in lockdown.

- Lockdown notification should be prioritized over the fire alarm notification. Why? During many active shooter incidents in schools, the fire alarm system was activated due to smoke from the firearm, making PA announcements inaudible throughout the building. This happened in Parkland, and we even saw it happen five years later in the Covenant Presbyterian shooting.

- A pre-recorded announcement needs to be made on the PA system advising all students, staff, and occupants: "We are in lockdown. Begin lockdown procedures. We are in lockdown." This message stays on a loop and in repeat mode every five seconds.

- All lockdown blue lights are triggered, alerting people who are hearing-impaired or inside of a loud space (like a band hall or gymnasium) that the school is in lockdown.

- All technology network-connected screen devices owned by the school district need to stop working and display "LOCKDOWN," including computers and TVs. This should force any user to stop what they are doing and would also prevent teachers from continuing to teach or watch a movie like what happened in Uvalde.

- All magnetically held doors connected to the fire alarm system should be released, forcing the doors to close. If allowed by state fire code, have these doors pre-locked to prevent ease of movement by the attacker. This will restrict their movement by creating a new obstacle and give more time for police response.

- All electronic access control needs to be shut down, and only select people with override cards or fobs should be able to have access. This reduces the chance an attacker could take a keycard off an injured staff and use it to bypass doors.

- All electronic or smart locks need to be engaged to a locked position.

- A mass notification needs to be sent to all parents or guardians advising them that the school is in lockdown and to *not* go to the school. This will ensure all first responders can get in and out of the scene quickly.

None of these actions happened in Uvalde or Parkland when the lockdown button was pushed, and lives could've been saved if they had. So much of this also relies on effective communication *during*

THE TEN COMMANDMENTS OF PREPARATION

the lockdown. One of the few products I don't mind publicly recommending is the Vocera system from Stryker Medical. It's an unbelievable device which allows staff to communicate to each other while other devices are in lockdown mode. Fair warning—it's expensive but worth it when lives are at stake.

6. DRILLS

Conducting lockdown drills and active shooter drills the proper way can save lives. Schools should not conduct a full-scale active shooter drill in a school during the school day with students present. Active shooter drills and active shooter training should instead be completed on Professional Development Days or when students are not present.

Full-scale active shooter drills have caused confusion for students and staff during a real attack. This was evident when hundreds of students and staff were standing in the hallway of the third floor of Parkland's Building 12 during the attack. They were getting ready to evacuate, thinking the attack was a drill. When Parkland teacher Ernest Rospierski was interviewed in the documentary *Inside Building 12*, he shared about how he thought it was a drill until he witnessed a student get shot and fall.

Schools should not be teaching students what to do during a real lockdown event. If you teach students your exact strategy for "Run, Hide, Barricade or Fight," most of the time you are teaching a future attacker your survival plans, which could give them the upper hand.

A joint study from FEMA and the Naval Postgraduate School's Center for Homeland Defense and Security found some disturbing proof for this. Looking at data from school shootings going back to 1970, they found that only about 20 percent of shooters had no

91

school affiliation whatsoever. Of the almost 80 percent who *did* have a school affiliation, a staggering *43 percent* were *current* students.[21]

As mentioned before, full-scale active shooter drills can traumatize children. The goal of a drill should never be to scare the school staff members or students into obedience. The goal is to give the students and staff a baseline for what is expected during an emergency. The training should always be empowering (see chapter 3, subsection "Training Students"), not fear-based.

When conducting a drill, it should always, *always* be clearly communicated that it is "only a drill" so staff and students can remain calm, just like when you do a fire drill. Schools should even go a step further to send out emails and texts when an emergency drill is being done.

In our work, we've heard stories of schools that did drills, and students thought it was a real emergency. Next thing you know, they're texting their parents about a lockdown situation, parents rush to the school, and they get into an accident on the way. Not only would this be a tragic event for the family, but once again, it's not worth the lawsuit that could result.

Like so many other things in life: communicate, communicate, communicate!

7. HARDENING LIFE OPENINGS TO THE ASTM F3561 STANDARD

Don't let the jargon on this one scare you away—I'll explain!

Every Life Opening (entry/exit) from the building and interior room doors and cross-corridor doorways should be hardened to the ASTM

---

21   Amy Rock, "K-12 School Shooting Statistics: 52 Years of Data," Campus Safety
       Magazine, October 5, 2023, accessed April 9, 2024, https://www.campussafety-
       magazine.com/safety/k-12-school-shooting-statistics-everyone-should-know/.

Forced-Entry-Resistance of Fenestration Systems after a Simulated Active Shooter Attack Standard, which is known as F3561. Why?

ASTM (American Society for Testing and Materials) is an independent testing company started in 1898. For over a century, they have been responsible for testing products for consumer safety. Later today, pick up some of the everyday products you use—computers, AirPods, smartphone—and look for the ASTM number. Essentially, they test to make sure these products are safe, that they're not going to catch on fire while you're using them and creates accountability for companies to make sure they're not lying to consumers.

It's one thing for a company to tell you, "Of course it's safe!" Well, of course they'll say that when they want you to buy it. It's another thing when a certified third-party company tells you.

If you're a school administrator or on a school board, here's something huge for you to know: *Companies are not required to use ASTM testing.* Plenty of companies take products to market which have *not* been ASTM tested; so any time you have a vendor come in and pitch a safety product to you, you should be asking, "Have the products passed ASTM standards?"

Fair warning: If you ever have Armoured One come to your school and ask me this question, I'll probably give you a hug.[22]

This hardening standard should include the door, glass, window film, vision lite kit, lock, handle, hardware, framing, and sidelights. This standard would have to be met when a new school building is being built or when these products are being upgraded or replaced.

---

22 As part of our mission, Armoured One is working to get ASTM testing passed as a minimum standard state mandate for products installed in public schools. We get some pushback on this from politicians who say it's "anti-business," especially since the window film companies can't pass the standards. Follow the money, and too often you'll see these same companies are paying lobbyists and donating to campaigns.

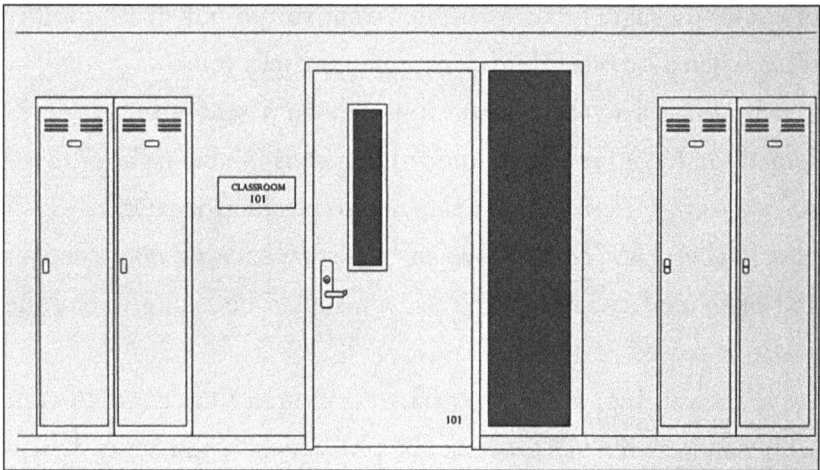

Note: Not all windows in the school or on the first floor need to be hardened to this standard, which can make the upgrade easier on the budget. Safety-conscious schools can definitely go overboard and waste money fortifying fewer essential areas. In the attacks where the glass and doors were shot, we see the attacker going to the door or sidelights adjacent to the door to make entry, so spending should be focused on hardening these specific windows first.

The evaluation process entails firing ten rounds from a .556 caliber AR15 rifle at the glass, followed by impacts from a one-hundred-pound ram starting at fifty-foot pounds of force. To meet the criteria for passing, the glass must endure the gunfire and subsequently withstand the ram impacts without the tip breaching the surface after two hits. The standard is structured into eight levels for assessment purposes.

Case in point, the attacker in Uvalde attempted to shoot victims *inside* their classrooms while he was outside, but he was unsuccessful in killing victims with this rare attack method. Hardening *every* window would actually be a waste of money, so invest that money into other security needs.

Remember, the NSSPA's case study of K–12 school shootings and active shooter indicates that the shooter is known to make entry into the school through a life opening about 99 percent of the time. This occurs via an unlocked door, entering naturally, or by attacking their way through. In some incidents, the shooter is admitted by staff because of a lack of training.

The attackers in some of the deadliest school shootings have also shot and/or attacked the door, door glass, or sidelights to make entry. It is also recommended that the ASTM Standard listed above be used for retrofitting existing doors, windows, frames, vision lite kits, and hardware. For new construction, we recommend a doorway with a tested assembly, meaning the entire door system is tested using the door slab, frame, hardware, glass, and vision lite kit.

To show just how essential this one measure is, see the following chart:

Location: Sandy Hook Elementary—Newtown, Connecticut
Incident Date: 12/14/12
Method of Entry: *Window next to the front doors*
Killed: 26
Injured: 2

Location: Marjory Stoneman Douglas High School—Parkland, Florida
Incident Date: 2/14/18
Method of Entry: *Classroom door glass*
Killed: 17
Injured: 17

Location: Central Visual & Performing Arts High School—St. Louis, Missouri
Date of Incident: 10/24/22
Method of Entry: *Side door glass/lower window*
Killed: 2
Injured: 7

Location: Covenant Presbyterian School—Nashville, Tennessee
Date of Incident: 3/27/23
Method of Entry: *Side door glass windows and classroom door glass*
Killed: 6
Injured: 0

Note 1: These are just *some* of the glass and doors that were shot out during attacks and account for over fifty murders. A full list could be its own book.

Note 2: For those who are interested in what legal measures could change this, see below for the bill language that should be passed in every state to create a minimal standard in glass and window film security.

Until we make ASTM F3561 a mandated standard, people will continue to die in attacks. And since it's not mandated, the companies who sell non-ASTM-tested products will be able to keep pleading ignorance.

8. LAW ENFORCEMENT ACCESS

If you live in a smaller district with a smaller police force, I highly recommend giving police a master key they can have on their keyring. In general, sworn local LEOs should have master keys to the exterior *and* interior doors of each school in their jurisdiction.

And if you are using electronic systems, then they should have electronic access override cards or fobs to all school buildings in their jurisdiction. Either way, we recommend that police and local LEOs have a master key in every patrol car.

Sometimes there are concerns from schools about what happens if a key gets lost. I prefer this line of thinking to the other end of the spectrum of giving out keys to anyone and everyone. We've seen school districts that were so free with handing out master keys, they had no idea *who* had them or *where* they all were.

So how do you mitigate this risk? After all, losing a master key not only makes you vulnerable—it also means you've got to rekey hundreds of classrooms, costing thousands of dollars. A cheap solution is to put an AirTag on these keys to know exactly where they are. If

---

23   "All new construction and renovation projects including, but not limited to, any improve-
      ments involving the replacement, upgrade, or security enhancement of exterior glazing
      at all glass panels on each entry door plus adjoining door and sidelight or adjacent
      window glass up to a height of seven feet above finished grade to have installed a clear
      window film or security glass that meets the ASTM F3561 'Standard Test Method for
      Forced-Entry-Resistance of Fenestration Systems After Simulated Active Shooter Attack'
      Test Standard to prevent individuals from entering the school building or room without
      authorization by breaking the glass in an exterior entry, door, or adjacent window."

one gets lost, you can track it down. This $30 expense can make you more secure *and* save $100,000 for a school district.

For small police agencies of less than fifty people, make sure you have a policy in place to document who has these and standard procedures about how they get turned in when someone leaves the department. They should be tested at least once a year to ensure they are in working condition. During an annual LEO campus walk-through is the perfect opportunity to do so.

Remember, you need to have it as part of your active shooter protocols for designated school staff to be able to meet police when they arrive and either let them in or hand them the key, like what happened with the Covenant Presbyterian shooting I described. Once again, you want to make sure you have multiple people designated with a master key since you never know which side of a school you'll need to be able to admit police.

Another recommended option is to install Knox boxes with master keys in them for police to access. These only require a punch code which could be given over radio. In an active shooter incident, your local LEOs may not be the first to respond—when the alert goes out, any nearby law enforcement could respond, including state troopers, FBI, or others who likely will not have a master key on hand.

This was the case in the Parkland shooting. Some of the first law enforcement to arrive were officers from Coral Springs, not Broward County where the school is located. Knox boxes are an easy, secure, and inexpensive solution for law enforcement access.

9. WAYFINDING

"Wayfinding" simply refers to making it easier for first responders to navigate your campus when they arrive. In chapter 3, we touched on the importance of using proper signage for first responders to use when they show up. Proper labeling and signage aids first responders to quickly respond to the incident and stop the shooter, treat victims, or evacuate a school.

For starters, label all buildings with the *name* of the school building. Place 24" × 24" signs with the building numbers on all sides of the building since first responders could be coming onto campus from any direction.

Next, number and label the entry/exits above each door in the building with a 12" × 12" sign. The label or sign should be on the interior and exterior *above* the door, unobstructed for visibility. The entries/exits should be numbered, starting with the main entrance (1) and going clockwise around the building. If there are multiple buildings on campus, label the building number and exit number on the signage. Example: *BLD 12, Exit 22.*

Clearly label all rooms in the building. We suggest the numbering you see below:

- *Basement – 000s or 0000s*
- *First Floor – 100s or 1,000s*
- *Second Floor – 200s or 2,000s*
- *Third Floor – 300s or 3,000s*

Numbering rooms based on the floor number is a simple and commonly used method across the commercial building industry, including in hotels, hospitals, and government buildings. Yet it's not always found in schools. If you have multiple buildings on campus, use the following example: *BLD 12, Room 226.*

An additional note on training is for staff to be fully trained on this numbering system and know how to use it. When a staff member is on the phone with 911 or on the radio with a LEO, they need to be able to say, "Shots were heard in Building 8," or, "He went into Room 117 in Building 1."

We *don't* want them saying, "Shots were heard in the band hall," or, "He went into Mr. Smith's classroom." Such directions will only slow down the first responder from doing their job and stopping the threat.

When conducting your staff training, one element should be a simple walk-through to get to know the building numbers, know where signage is located, know where all entry/exits are located. In fact, this should be part of any new staff training, not only your annual active shooter training. Additionally, we strongly recommend training staff with a mock phone call. Give them a randomized scenario where they have to then give directions using only the numbering system.

One note specific to EMS: In the same way you invite your local LEOs to do a walk-through to learn the campus, it's a good idea to do the same with your local EMS. Even though they won't begin their work until the attacker has been neutralized, the faster they can reach any injured individuals, the more likely those people can be saved.

Likewise, ask EMS to explain to you their system for getting wounded in and out of the building so that, if the worst happens, you can assist them in moving faster to save lives. You can make this part of your staff training by having a local EMS representative come in and discuss their procedures.

10. TEMPORARY CONCEALMENT BLINDS

Finally, develop a quick and effective way to cover windows for classrooms or other room with students or staff. Drop Down or Lockdown Blinds are available to block the view of the attacker. This measure should work in conjunction with hardening glass to the ASTM F-3561 and barricading the door.

Temporary concealment blinds should:

- Be made of high-quality blackout fabric.

- Include a weighted hem-bar to keep it in place.

- Be capable of quick deployment during lockdown situations.

- Be fire-retardant as needed.

At the price point of this one safety measure, this should be mandated. For most schools, it only costs a few thousand dollars to install these dropdown blinds, which takes away the sight line from the shooter.

While these concealment blinds won't stop bullets, past attacks have demonstrated that attackers are attempting to get into rooms where they *know* people are inside. As difficult as this is to fathom, they want to *see* who they are attempting to kill. Taking away a visual of a potential victim can help save lives. In the Parkland shooting, lives were saved on the second floor when teachers barricaded and covered their windows.

FOLLOWING THE RULES

Before you move on, re-read the opening story for this chapter. Look at how many of these "commandments" were followed which slowed down the attacker and successfully protected every single student and staff member in the school. When schools take the right actions with the right training, protocols, and safety measures, it protects everyone—and makes it easier for law enforcement to do their sworn duty.

Unfortunately, Uvalde shows us what happens when there is slow police response—or rather, a lack of police response. But if the schools had followed even half of these rules, lives could still have been saved. The rules work when you follow them.

So far, the bulk of our conversation has focused on preparation because it's the key element in staying one step ahead. Now it's time to turn our attention to what you do when the unthinkable happens, and what actions need to occur when an attacker arrives and you go into lockdown.

|5|

WHAT TO DO
WHEN THE
WORST HAPPENS

When I went to Nashville to investigate the Covenant Presbyterian shooting and see what we could learn, I spoke with Wynonna, the kitchen coordinator, about her experience. She described how even though they are a smaller school, the fire alarm was so loud, she couldn't even hear the shots, so it was her husband, the head of facilities management, who told her they were in lockdown. Immediately, she hid in the kitchen, barricaded the door, and covered the window.

"We trained for this," she said. "They taught us everything we needed to know … We never thought we'd have to use it." I asked her what advice she'd give to staff in other schools, and she said, "Pay attention to your active shooter trainings. It'll save your life."

Tim Kennedy expressed the idea best when he said, "You don't rise to the moment but rather fall to the level of your training."[24]

---

24   Tim Kennedy, *Scars and Stripes: An Unapologetically American Story of Fighting the Taliban, UFC Warriors, and Myself*, read by the author (New York: Atria Books, 2022), Audible audio ed., 15 hr., 52 min.

No one wants to think a shooting could happen at their school. As a dad to two kids who are still in school, I know I don't. If you abide by the measures I've laid out, we have the data to show it works. Schools that implement these measures are stopping incidents. It's too bad more of these victory stories *don't* make the headlines. If only the media would flood a town every time a school successfully *prevents* an attack … but that's a conversation for another book.

We need to turn our focus now to look beyond the right preparation to the *right actions* in the midst of an active shooter event. Even with the other problems that happened in Uvalde, lives still could have been saved if the right actions had been taken during the attack—both from the school *and* from law enforcement.

Throughout this chapter, you'll notice many callbacks to preventative actions to show the connection between the two. If some information feels repetitive, it's on purpose—these are details worthy of reminder.

First, we'll look at what actions schools need to take in the midst of an active shooter event. Then, we'll turn our attention to what law enforcement and first responders need to do. Finally, we'll talk about what parents and community members need to do whenever they find out about a lockdown situation.

SCHOOL RESPONSE

The Covenant Presbyterian School shooting in Nashville is an interesting case study of the right actions to take. I say this because the best preventative action they took was training their staff well. After all, they had nothing good in place for security—a lousy lockdown system. The shooter shot out the glass and walked right in. If they'd also had better physical security, I feel confident they would have had no deaths.

One special note to make here is how one of the attacker's friends attempted to call for help after they received a message about the shooter's intention to attack the school and then commit suicide. Unfortunately, it was too late when this message came in, but it's indicative these young people knew the *right* response to make in the moment, which deserves recognition. Looking back at the last chapter (see Commandment #2), this is exactly why schools need assessment teams and systems in place for students to make reports when their friends make dangerous remarks.

No matter your job title, the most important thing you can do is to *follow the training*. Assuming, of course, that you're using the right training as previously discussed. At Covenant Presbyterian, they used "Run, Hide, Barricade, Fight," and it worked *incredibly* well.

When the shooter shot out the glass in the school's entry, it sent up enough smoke to set off the fire alarm system. A teacher on the second floor began to evacuate the classroom because of the fire alarm, which unfortunately resulted in kids entering the hallway, putting them in the shooter's line of fire. Also, with the fire alarm squealing, it was more difficult to hear the lockdown alert, so it's understandable why the teacher thought she needed to get the kids out of the classroom.

This is why I'll continue to advocate for all staff to be trained to "stop, look, listen, and smell" before they move out of a safe classroom into a hallway when a fire alarm is going off. Instead of a blaring fire alarm, the warning needs to be a voice notification letting them know "the fire alarm has been activated." This provides an opportunity for staff to hear what is going on beyond the screaming alarm. It also allows for better communication from staff to students.

The lockdown alert also needs to be a voice notification and not an alarm sound to remove any confusion. These systems can also work in tandem with one another. An example would be a recorded voice saying, "Lockdown, begin lockdown procedure immediately. The fire alarm has also been activated. Follow lockdown procedure." Your lockdown procedure needs to address the fire alarm scenario, letting staff know that they need to safely evacuate *only* if absolutely necessary, that is, if a fire or smoke is present in their room.

A similar situation happened in Parkland when gunshots caused ceiling tile dust to set off the fire alarm. This is why, if you can afford it, the blue lockdown lights are so essential. In the event of a fire alarm going off during the lockdown, the blue lights serve as another safeguard to communicate, "No, this is a lockdown, not a fire evacuation."

Another right action taken by Covenant Presbyterian was how they had a staff member ready to hand keys over to law enforcement—and give instructions about the shooter's whereabouts so Officer Engelbert and Officer Collazo could move quickly.

Whatever information you can give to 911 or the responding officers, do so immediately and in clear language. The more information they have about the shooter's whereabouts, the sooner the attacker can be apprehended.

SCHOOL RESOURCE OFFICERS (SROS)

During an active shooter scenario, there's only one staff member who should be heading toward the shooter—your SRO.

In the last chapter, I talked about how the school board had pushed back against adding an armed SRO to their schools. In a 2021 study by Homeland Security looking into averted school attacks, they found that an SRO had played an active role in preventing the plot in *31 percent* of the cases.[25] Sometimes, schools and parents are afraid to have SROs because they think the SRO's job is to arrest kids—but SROs are there to keep kids *safe*. That could mean breaking up a fight now and then, but more importantly, it means being ready for the worst.

An important detail here is for them to be *permanent* SROs. In Uvalde, they had SROs, but they were non-permanent, meaning they had four floating between eight campuses. Likewise, Parkland had only one between twelve buildings.

Once lockdown is called, the SRO needs to immediately spring into action and run *toward* the gunshots to get there as quickly as possible. Besides their firearm, they should have their vest on, police radio, phone, tac-med kit, and school radio. I advise SROs to have their firearm and vest on at all times. Believe me, I know how uncomfortable and hot they get, but every second you're having to pull it on is a second a child could be shot.

Frankly, SROs need to keep in good physical shape, too. I'm not saying you need to look like an Olympic wrestler, but if you're in a three-hundred-thousand-square-foot building and the shooter is on the opposite end, that's two minutes to get to them even at a sprint. You need to be fit enough so you're not exhausted before you even have to confront a shooter.

SROs must be true warriors—compassionate and loving but ready to protect and fight. Teachers and students didn't swear an oath, but *you* did. Your mentality should be, "I'm going to have the bullets fired at me, so they aren't fired at staff and students. And I'm going to do all I can to stop this shooter."

---

25   Lina Alathari et al., "Averting Targeted School Violence: A U.S. Secret Service Analysis of Plots against Schools," National Threat Assessment Center, March 2021, 51. https://www.secretservice.gov/sites/default/files/reports/2021-03/USSS%20 Averting%20Targeted%20School%20Violence.2021.03.pdf.

If you're an SRO or a school admin reading this, one of the suggestions I give most often is to invest in a fingerprint-secured safe with a Level-3 ballistic vest and a rifle. I know schools are concerned about a rifle being on premises—they're worried someone could break in and steal it. But during an active shooter situation, you don't want your SRO having to run out to their car to grab a rifle—it's actually less secure in the car than it would be if you follow these easy measures:

- Get a fingerprint safe so only authorized people can open it up. If you've got a six-hundred-pound safe mounted in place, it's not walking away.

- Install an alarm specifically on the SRO's office door.

- Disguise the safe. Make it look like cabinets or conceal it in some other way.

When you consider the average police response time for active shooter events is eight minutes, having an armed SRO cuts the response down to ninety seconds. This is a huge difference, which is why I'll continue to advocate for them. Yes, I have seen some SROs who fail in the line of duty—like in Parkland where he went outside and aimed the gun at the building. But statistically, you're still better off with one than without.

LAW ENFORCEMENT/FIRST RESPONDERS

On that note, it's time to switch gears to how law enforcement should respond. Once again, we see an incredible example with the Covenant Presbyterian response. Something for first responders to keep in mind when arriving at a school is that it's possible you take fire from the shooter as you're arriving, so have your eyes peeled. This happened in Nashville with the shooter breaking a window and firing at the nearest police car, and we saw something similar with the Las Vegas shooting where the attacker was shooting down from above as law enforcement arrived.

During an event, most of the communication needs to be coming from school staff, *not from you*. It's not necessary for you to tell staff what you're doing over the radio—just listen to their directions so you can move faster. When you need to communicate with any other officers or EMS, keep your language simple and clear—the time for codes is gone.

If you have enough officers to do so, an officer should be posted outside the school to keep the roads clear so that backup and EMS can get through. They should communicate with the school to know where to direct any parents or other community members who show up.

Once the attacker is neutralized, focus must immediately shift to finding anyone who is injured. Your job is to work with school staff to get victims out as fast as possible so everyone can be accounted for, especially if some classes evacuated or if some kids fled as we saw happen with Sandy Hook.

A key note here for police—let the school take charge of this process. I was recently at a school in Florida that had gone into lockdown. Thankfully, it ended up being a false alarm, but they had evacuated around three thousand students, and it was over one hundred degrees outside. The police were directing the staff and students and sent them to gather on the football field out under the blazing sun. Soon, kids were passing out and having seizures. Meanwhile, police were trying to manage the pickup process as parents arrived, and it became a chaotic scene.

The school administrators asked me what they could've done differently, so I said, "When it's safe, you take charge. It's your school." School staff are much better equipped to pick one or two secondary indoor locations which are ready at all times—whether it's a nearby church, a government building, or whatever else is within safe walking distance as mentioned in chapter 4.

Law enforcement, I'm one of you. Believe me, I know the feeling of needing to take charge during a dangerous situation, especially when you've had the training. But remember, it's your job to serve and protect the *community*. Once the danger has passed, you need to let teachers and staff be in charge of the kids. Let them decide where the best place is to gather everyone and how pickup should work. It's what they do every day.

In the meantime, you can be working with designated staff to look for any children who are missing or who may still be hiding because they don't realize the incident is over—or because they may be in shock. Do a methodical search of the building with participation from school staff. Even if you know the layout of the building from doing a walk-through, staff are more likely to know which nooks and crannies a child might hide in.

Also, ensure that your 911 centers have been properly trained with a protocol for *reverse 911 calls*. That is, when 911 receives a call about suspicious behavior or another violent attack near a school, then they should be calling the closest school to warn them. You see this happen a lot in urban communities when there is an armed robbery—911 will contact other businesses in the area to let them know so they can take preventative actions. Unfortunately, this is a training gap for many dispatch centers, including in Uvalde.

Around 11:21 a.m., the attacker shot his grandmother. At 11:23 a.m., a neighbor called 911 to report the shooting since the grandmother had survived and walked outside. Despite the fact they were only a quarter mile from the school, no reverse 911 call was made to warn the school. Five minutes later, the gunman showed up, crashed his grandfather's truck, and began his attack. In those five minutes, the kids on the playground could have been evacuated, the lockdown button pushed and communicated, and the exterior door locked correctly.

So, if you're a school administrator or on a school board, connect with your local 911 center and ask if they have a reverse 911 call policy and hold them accountable to train their staff on it.

After the Covenant Presbyterian shooting, I visited with Chief Drake in Nashville and got a giant hug from him. He knew I'd already been dealing with Uvalde for close to a year by then, and we were both grieved about the failures in the police response. Referring to the incredible work of his own team, he said, "My men and women trained twelve years for those fourteen minutes."

You never know when or where "those fourteen minutes" are going to happen. The best you can do is to prepare, prepare, prepare through training and talking with your local schools. During an incident, your job is to protect, protect, protect by acting swiftly and communicating clearly. If you can do that, you'll save lives and be able to hold your head high for keeping your oath.

PARENTS AND THE COMMUNITY

Another problem with Uvalde which was well-publicized was the number of parents and community members who showed up at Robb Elementary School. Rightfully, they were shouting at police to do their jobs—especially given the fact nearly four hundred officers responded. A video posted on YouTube showed police restraining an adult who wanted to run into the school.

While there is no excuse for the inaction from law enforcement in Uvalde, it teaches us that the presence of parents and community members at the scene of the crime only creates additional chaos. This underlies a failure of communication by both the school and law enforcement, who should have been redirecting parents and community members away from the scene and to a designated pickup location.

The same way that automated texts and calls should be sent out about the lockdown, these should be followed with directions for parents and relevant community members. Update them as you learn new information through mass texts and posts on social media. For example:

"For the safety of your child and yourself, please do NOT come to the school. Head to secondary location X and await information on pickup."

If you look up pictures from Sandy Hook, you'll see a similar chaotic scene—cars lined up and down the street, including media vehicles, all obstructing the movement of EMS and law enforcement. As a parent myself, I understand the need to get to your child, to find out where they are. But in an active shooter scenario, you'll only make the situation worse with your presence.

Most importantly, you don't want to obstruct EMS and police, but also, you don't want community members accidentally trampling on evidence at the school. Investigation happens as soon as the situation is static, and law enforcement need to be able to scope the grounds to learn what happened—and whether there may still be any threat. For example, what if the shooter planted a secondary explosive device to go off afterward? Or what if there is another shooter who was coordinating to come in later?

As school administrators redirect parents to the secondary pickup location, you also need to be coordinating with other community members. For instance, clergy members may need to be redirected to the secondary location so they can tend to members of their congregation or counsel others in need. Or you may need to communicate with the local transportation authority to get city buses to the school to evacuate children to the secondary location.

Work with police to identify victims as best as possible so you can quickly communicate with their parents. Back during the Columbine shooting, there was a particularly tragic story of a father who didn't know his son was dead until the next day, when he learned from the newspaper.

Call your local hospitals and also give them relevant information—they will likely be overloaded with calls from community members asking if their loved ones have been brought in. You need to have a liaison working with the hospital to help identify those students and connect them with their families quickly.

PREPARATION IS THE KEY

Alexander Graham Bell once said, "Before anything else, preparation is the key to success."[26] Think about all that we prepare for in life—job interviews, competitions, weddings, starting a business, and on and on. Why? Because when you prepare, you know what to do in real time when the rubber meets the road.

When it comes to school safety, this is doubly true. Remember—the key is to stay one step ahead of an active shooter. How will you know what to do if you have not prepared? I'll continue to preach this far and wide, because the better you prepare, the less likely you face an active shooter situation. But even if you do, at least then you'll know what to do to save lives.

It's an imperfect world we live in, though. So, what do you do *after* an attack? How do you even begin to pick up the pieces? What are the right steps to take to start healing as a community and address both the individual and collective trauma?

---

26 Brainy Quote, "Alexander Graham Bell Quotes," BrainyQuote.com, accessed April 2, 2024, https://www.brainyquote.com/quotes/alexander_graham_bell_387728.

6

THE AFTERMATH

Being a cop or detective is nothing like what you see on TV or in movies. Believe me, it would be fun to catch the bad guy before the rampage, have no paperwork, and then be home by 7:00 p.m. Such is the fairy tale life of police work only possible on TV.

What they don't show are the terrible, heartbreaking days that push you to the brink of physical, mental, emotional, and spiritual exhaustion. Days where you lose friends who are like family—killed in the line of duty or even committing suicide. The one commonality with all these types of days is a *lot* of paperwork and hours away from your family.

My primary trigger for my own personal PTSD is when children are injured or killed. The crimes we witnessed on our job as police officers and detectives were bad, but the death and abuse of children was the worst. Mentally preparing to go to Uvalde triggered my PTSD, and I became very short with my wife on the day of the attack. Deep down, I knew what I would be facing for the next several months.

Because she's an absolute angel, Maria immediately comforted me, understanding my crabbiness was my PTSD expressing itself. I try to be this tough former cop, but deep down, I'm a regular dad and husband who wishes I could make these shootings stop.

I started crying as my little 5'2" wife held me. I felt like a failure because I wondered if Armoured One could have prevented this massacre. We started the company to stop shootings, but here we were again. Not only another school shooting but an *elementary* school.

Much of what we do after a shooting is for free or highly discounted for schools. It is a constant go, go, go life post-shooting. It's time to serve others while seeking answers. Only then can we stay one step ahead of the next shooting.

The next morning, I flew to San Antonio, and then the drive to Uvalde was about ninety miles. By then, it was pretty well-known that the Uvalde police had let the shooter stay in two classrooms for more than twenty minutes. There were reports that the SRO and a police officer had shot at the suspect from outside and missed him, but I still could not believe a fellow police officer would not run into that room and confront the shooter. This is literally what we had been taught to do ever since Columbine.

During the drive, my phone was ringing nonstop. Between Armoured One and ONE Training, we work with thousands of schools and law enforcement agencies across the country. Most of them know that we have someone on scene within twenty-four hours of a shooting, so they wanted answers: How did so many die? Why didn't the police immediately respond? How did the shooter get in? These school administrators and law enforcement personnel were calling me for answers because they were eager to prevent the same from happening to them. Frankly, it sucked not having answers to give them yet.

Maria called me the minute I passed the City of Uvalde sign on US 90. My stomach sank, and I was fighting the tears when my phone rang. Either she was watching my Life360 app or she's just that in tune with my heart. She said, "I love you, Thomas. I am so proud that you have not given up this fight. Those families in Uvalde need you, the school district needs you, and you need to be there. I love you—now go fight with everything you have to stop the next shooter!" God knew it was what I needed at that moment.

As I entered Uvalde, it was clear this was a primarily Mexican city. My wife Maria is Mexican and Irish. My mother-in-law is Mexican and from Texas, bilingual in Spanish and English, and has taught me a lot about Mexican heritage—especially the incredible food. My youngest two children are spitting images of their mother, and it felt more like me going home to my family.

After I turned onto Geraldine Street near the school, I was directed by police to park at the end of the road, which was already packed with media. You literally had to push past them to get a view of the school.

(Uvalde) Geraldine St. near S. Piper Ln. at around 11:30 a.m. The day after the shooting. This is about three blocks from the school. Most of these vehicles are with the media or LEO.

We need to take a closer look at what happens immediately after an active shooter event. You especially need to see how law enforcement approaches the investigation—and also how to be wary of messages from both the media and politicians, who may not have the full story and have their own agendas.

Whether you're an educator, law enforcement, or a parent, you have to be cautious with the information coming from a scene. So first, let's take a closer look at the investigation process so you can better understand what law enforcement is doing in the crucial first few days after a shooting.

INDEPENDENT INVESTIGATION

In the aftermath, there are more questions than answers. It's easy for rumors to get reported on the news—and it's rare that the media go back to correct any misinformation. They just carry on presenting the latest update. But even the greatest investigative journalists can only do so much on the investigation front.

As a homicide detective, I had to learn to look for the details no one else saw and ask the questions no one else thought about. I still use these skills when Armoured One does our own independent investigating after an incident.

So much of the investigation comes down to talking with as many people as possible. No one has the full story, so you have to get as many angles as possible, find the overlaps, and piece it all together.

It's like if you sent a group of people to a baseball game, but some of them show up late and some of them leave early, and all of them have different seats. Not all of them will remember every detail of the game depending on when they arrived, left, or got up from their seats to go grab food. If someone wasn't at the game at all, you can usually figure it out because they are only able to repeat what everyone knows about the game from watching it on TV. They don't have the same level of detail.

After taking some pictures for our investigation, I made my way out to meet some of the first responders. One of our company connections is tied in very well to the Texas Department of Public Safety (DPS). The news America was seeing at the time reported that the local police and school resource officers got into a gunfight with the suspect outside of the school. Our DPS connection was the first to confirm this was *not* true, and he didn't know how this information had hit the news or the governor's office.

Many of the local Uvalde police were tight-lipped at first and wouldn't engage with me. In fact, they didn't even want us there, which was a huge red flag. At many other shooting scenes we visit, our presence is welcomed by local law enforcement because it's not uncommon for us to have contacts they need. Plus they know we can help with the investigation.

Even though the Uvalde police weren't talking, others on the scene were more open. I met a deputy from Zavala County Sheriff's Office who confirmed that law enforcement entry to the room was not made into the classrooms for over *seventy* minutes.

From there, I walked the perimeter of the scene a few times and met victims' family members. It was heartbreaking learning about the different victims of this tragedy. I met aunts, uncles, grandparents, and cousins of victims, all in disbelief.

While making my way around Robb Elementary, I also met some of the first responders who went into the building during the attack. One of them told me he arrived at the scene about thirty minutes after the shooter entered the building. He was furious that he was not allowed near the actual shooting scene. Instead, he had been placed on an outer perimeter. Like me, he was also in disbelief when he heard that police had not made entry to the classroom.

His wife knew one of the victim's family, so he began to tear up and said, "I can't forgive myself for staying on the outer perimeter. I should've disobeyed orders. I should have just left my post and gone into the school."

Story after story, I heard multiple people say they wanted to do more, but they were trusting that the police on scene were already doing everything they could. They had the same bad assumption I've had to grapple with—that law enforcement will always do what they're supposed to.

Now, I knew I needed to find someone who had been *inside* the fourth-grade building during the attack. I needed to hear for myself why police did not confront the shooter sooner. I had been retired from LEO for over four years, but I knew standard active shooter training from 2018 was teaching officers to run into a building and confront the shooter without delay.

In an investigation, you can learn a lot from those who were nearby, so I knocked on doors and attempted to speak to as many witnesses as possible. Some residents were already sick of all the journalists around and did not answer the door. Others did not speak enough English for me to communicate well with them. Google Translate can only get you so far.

But some people did answer and were willing to talk. I met a sweet, older woman who lives directly across the street from Robb Elementary's main entrance and welcomed me into her house with open arms. She fought back tears as she told me her great-granddaughter was in school during the attack. The great grandma told me that she was in the school a short time before the attack to attend a class ceremony for her great-granddaughter. From her, I learned how the school would prop open exterior doors, especially when it was cool outside in the morning, like it was on May 24, 2022. She shared how she entered the school for the ceremony through a propped-open door.

This confirmed another problem in Uvalde—the school not following their own protocols with locked doors. And why? Because it was more convenient to prop open the door. But always remember, if it's convenient for you, it's convenient for a shooter.

She went on to tell me she came home from the ceremony and was cleaning when she saw a police officer run by. At first, she assumed it was because of an illegal immigrant bailout nearby since these happened often. She did not think it had anything to do with the school because she never heard a lockdown alarm or an announcement—and she constantly heard the bells and announcements from the school given the proximity. In fact, as we spoke, the school bell rang, and it was clear as day sitting in her house. No doubt in my mind she would have heard a lockdown alarm if there had been one. This was a new detail I hadn't yet heard from anyone else.

After she saw a cop run by, she locked the door. Looking out the window, she saw tons of police responding to the school, so she attempted to call her granddaughter to tell her that something terrible was happening at the school. Thank God her great-granddaughter lived, but sadly her neighbor's niece was one of the teachers killed. This is exactly why schools need counselors or chaplains available at all times. So many forgotten victims are suffering from PTSD even though their family members lived.

Our goal is to talk to as many people as possible to put the puzzle together. So, I even sat down with Rolando, the shooter's grandfather. He's a sweet and caring man in his seventies, and I sat on the living room couch, my feet on the ground where the shooter had slept from February 2022 until the day of the attack.

As I spoke with Rolando, I assured him that he and his wife were victims of this tragedy, too. His voice cracked, and his eyes filled with tears as he said, "Mijo (Spanish term of endearment for his grandson) shot my wife, Sally, that day. Even though she lived, we both died right then. He was the devil that day, and I hate what he did."

Rolando was so broken, telling me how devastated he was, how much he loved Uvalde, and how he knew some of the families who had lost their loved ones. From him, we got a better picture of the shooter—how his father was never really in the picture and how his mother had raised him. This is an all-too-common story for school active shooters.

It was just three months before when the shooter's mom had dropped him off at Rolando and Sally's place. Rolando described his daughter as a hardworking mom—until she got hooked on meth and her life fell apart. I could tell that Rolando loved his daughter but hated what she had turned into from the drug use.

They didn't have much room, so the shooter slept on the living room floor. As it turned out, Sally had worked for the Uvalde Consolidated Independent School District (CISD) for over twenty-five years and loved the school kids. Rolando said that her heart was more destroyed by what their grandson did to them than when he shot her in the face.

Some reports have claimed the grandparents provided the guns to the suspect—but this is wrong. Rolando is strictly anti-gun and never allowed guns or ammo in his house. He said his grandson knew this and had sneaked around behind his back to get firearms. Rolando thought his grandson was saving money to get an apartment—not to buy guns for a rampage.

He shared that his grandson was not as mean or terrible as the newspapers were saying. He told me that the shooter was a sweet boy growing up but had drastically changed in the past year. Rolando stated that the shooter must have been doing stuff on his phone (social media) because they saw nothing of his plans, no signs to report to police. He told me that if he had any indication that his grandson was going to attack the school, he would have reported it. Seeing the pain in his eyes, I believed him.

We began to talk about the day of the attack, which he said had been a normal one until he received the call that his wife had been shot. According to him, his grandson got angry with his grandmother over being removed from their cell phone plan. He went outside, then closed himself into the bedroom, making noise—which Rolando believes was when he loaded the gun. Sally kept knocking on the door, telling him to open it. When he finally did, he pointed a rifle in her face and shot her.

Sally pretended to be dead, afraid he would shoot her again. On the ground, she heard him looking for Rolando's truck keys even though he did not have a license or know how to drive. Once he found the keys, he stole the truck and drove off.

Somehow, Sally was able to get up onto her feet, made her way outside, and then the neighbor across the street called 911 for help. It would be about a minute later when the shooter crashed the truck outside of Robb Elementary.

I could see that Rolando was grateful someone was listening to him. Many people would seek to blame them since the shooter was able to buy and hide guns while under their roof. But they were only a direct influence on the shooter for the three months he was living with them. And many kids hide something from their parents— drugs, alcohol, boyfriends or girlfriends, depression, suicide, and so much more. I gave Rolando a hug before I left, and we've kept in touch to this day.

Being on scene in Uvalde gave our team an opportunity to find out *how* it all happened. We were able to release our first Uvalde Debrief Report to schools and law enforcement nationwide within *seven days* of the attack. As new information came out, we updated the original report, which is normal since some details aren't available until released by the courts. But our findings were later validated by the Department of Justice's own investigation into Uvalde which came out more than eighteen months later.

While I hate how long these official reports take to come out, I know the reasons why. The law can be very specific about what can be counted as admissible evidence, so investigators must exert extraordinary due diligence in what they collect and ensure it will hold up in court. The reason Armoured One is able to release our findings so quickly is because we're not collecting evidence for court—our goal is to educate schools and law enforcement as soon as possible to save lives in any future incidents.

We behave more like a private investigator does. We have no official jurisdiction—we can't bring people in for questioning or issue warrants. Nor do we want to. Since we're not law enforcement, we're able to get people talking to us who might be more guarded with police, especially if they don't have a positive view of LEOs. We operate from a place of human compassion, not forced compliance.

Still, hopefully, this can give you a picture of how investigations are carried out, how much work is involved in gathering information, fact-checking it, and putting together a complete narrative of the event. But before we move on, here are some additional aspects of investigation from a law enforcement perspective you should be aware of.

LAW ENFORCEMENT INVESTIGATION

It's important to keep in perspective that investigation tactics can vary whether it's local police, sheriff's office, the FBI, or any other law enforcement organization. Different jurisdictions have different rules they have to follow, especially depending on the type of crime being investigated. So, the information in this section looks at what is broadly true for investigations but specifically with regard to active shooter incidents.

First off, law enforcement is going to secure the scene following the attack. In part, this is to preserve as much evidence as possible, such as shell casings, footprints, blood, fingerprints, and review any video surveillance from camera systems to piece together exactly what happened. All of this evidence is essential whether there will be a trial or not. As we've seen time after time, even when a shooter is killed during the attack, trials can still happen—such as civil suits against the school, against the state, or even against anyone who may have helped the shooter carry out their attack.

But a major reason for securing the scene is that they need to see if anyone is still inside the building, hiding or injured. If injured, they need to get them out as fast and safely as possible so EMS can do their lifesaving work and transport victims to area hospitals. Also, if there were deaths, then law enforcement has the unpleasant job of finding the bodies, preserving any evidence from the bodies, and beginning the difficult work of IDing the victims.

This is one area where law enforcement can continue to improve. Too often, we see stories of parents who are anxiously waiting to find out where their child is—they don't know if they have been killed or if they are at a hospital being treated. And since the victims often don't have IDs on them, hospitals are also at a loss for who they are treating. Law enforcement needs to be working with teachers and school staff at this point to help in quickly identifying the bodies and alerting the families quickly.

After this—or sometimes concurrently if there are adequate resources—investigators head to wherever the shooter lived to document any evidence there. They must be cautious with this since the shooter may have dangerous items in their home, such as bomb-making kits. But investigators are looking into any written plans which might reveal motive or how the shooter planned their attack.

In the aftermath of Columbine, investigators discovered the shooters had been practicing out in the woods near their home. Knowing this helps investigators find out who else they need to talk to and whether anyone else was involved in planning the attack. Is there still a threat to the school if a second attacker is at large? Was there any neglect which led to the shooter being able to carry out their attack? Were there warning signs which should have been reported?

These insights lead to further questions being asked by law enforcement, some of them more introspective: "How did we allow this to happen? What warning signs did we miss?" Often, investigations will expose gaps in reporting and flaws in police work.

For example, with the Parkland investigation, it was uncovered that police had dealt with the shooter *over forty times* prior to the attack—and also, it was found that the school district hadn't turned over all of the information about the shooter, including one report which described his potential to be "the next active shooter." Had there been better communication—from both sides—the threat could have been assessed and dealt with *before* an attack happened.

Depending on an agency's jurisdiction, they can also subpoena individuals and bring them in for questioning to learn more. Along the way, all of the information is being documented—or at least, it's supposed to be. But everything has to be verified so it can hold up in the court of law—which requires time.

Also, it's common for there to be multiple investigations. Local police may be doing one, state police, FBI, and whoever else needs to be involved. Sometimes, these groups collaborate and share information. Other times, these groups can be very competitive, so they don't always share info with each other—though it would be better if they did. Sometimes, when a contradiction is uncovered, it can help open up a new lead.

Some information may be released to the public if investigators feel it will help them get more information by prompting someone else to come forward. But much of what they find will be kept confidential because they never want to do anything which could compromise a future trial. Certainly, this can lead to frustration among the community that simply wants answers, and it can feel like investigators are being cagey. While I can empathize with this personally and agree some investigations and reports take far too long, in general, I encourage patience with the process. It's always better to end up with *confirmed* evidence and true information, not guesses or speculation. Which brings us to the role the media plays in the aftermath …

THE MEDIA IMPACT

When I headed to Uvalde the day after the shooting, I landed in San Antonio about 9:45 a.m. While in line for my rental car, I saw men who clearly worked for a national news network. Nowadays, these shooting scenes become a media frenzy as the most famous news anchors in the world are typically on-site within twenty-four to thirty-six hours of the attack.

With Uvalde, it helped that I had been to so many school shootings because I knew a few journalists and their security teams. One national journalist whom I'd met a few times greeted me when we saw each other and allowed me into their tent so I could get a better view of the school.

Look, I'm not here to demonize everyone in the media—I've met some great journalists like David Muir and Anderson Cooper who are fantastic at what they do and seem to have their hearts in the right place. The media is going to do their job no matter what, whether it's reporting on an accident or an election, so I have nothing against individuals doing their jobs.

But such stories end up being a major money maker for the news outlets. I've personally witnessed them pay homeowners $10,000 a week to use their yard to film in front of the school. Don't ever forget that when a major school attack happens, news agencies and politicians are the ones who are immediately making money and benefiting.

The political left is often seen fighting for gun reform and even eliminating the Second Amendment. Then, you've got the political right fighting to protect gun owners and their right to bear arms. Politicians make money by getting on the news and saying they are fighting to remove guns—or protect them, depending on which side they fall on. Then, people who align with that politician's views will donate money to their campaign to help them fight for removing guns or protecting them. Since nothing has really changed with the Second Amendment since Columbine in 1999, the only ones benefiting from the ongoing argument are the politicians themselves.

Meanwhile, since every network wants to be the first to deliver a scoop, they can end up reporting information that hasn't been fact-checked. Or even worse, they find out the names of victims and report it on air before parents have even been notified. Instead, they should be showing respect to the families and make sure it's okay to release the names.

Also, some people just want to be on TV. This is where we get "Teenage Tales," where students will share their stories—but sometimes, they weren't even at the school when the attack happened. This happened in Parkland with a student who was interviewed by multiple media outlets, providing a "firsthand account" of the attack—but it turned out he was nowhere near Building 12 when the shooting occurred.

Another area where I'd like to see the media change their practices more is with how they report on the shooter. They unwittingly make these shooters famous—which is what the shooter wanted—and which only inspires more shooters later. After the Aurora, Colorado, cinema shooting in 2012, parents of the victims started a campaign called "No Notoriety" to push against the unintentional glorification of shooters in the media. Other groups like Don't Name Them are doing the same work, advocating to "shift the media focus from the suspects who commit these acts to the victims, survivors, and heroes who stop them."[27]

The money-making potential of these stories can also compromise the quality of the investigation, even if this isn't their intent. Back at our headquarters, we have people scanning the news for witnesses we might need to talk to in the investigation. Sometimes, when we track them down and ask for a conversation, the response is, "Well, what's the incentive?"

When I get this question, I always say, "To save lives."

For some people, this works. But for those who are looking for a media payday, they'll say, "Nah, I don't feel like talking." Perhaps they

---

27   Don't Name Them, "Home," DontNameThem.org, accessed March 14, 2024, https://www.dontnamethem.org/.

don't really have any information of value—but what if they do? What if they know something which could help the investigation? But now they're not willing to talk unless there is cash involved.

In poorer communities like Uvalde, people can easily get taken advantage of. For some families of victims and survivors, they simply can't turn down the offer, especially if they are about to be faced with steep medical or therapy bills. So, they take the money in exchange for their child being re-traumatized by sharing their story.

Don't get me wrong—I'm not saying the media doesn't have a role. What they should be doing is working with law enforcement by sharing any information they learn in an interview right away, instead of law enforcement having to learn from the news and then track someone down again. They should also be working with school officials to help get out the word for any important updates, such as secondary pickup locations.

A related problem is how politicians use the media to push an agenda—or make themselves look good. I recently saw this happen with a Southern state where they made a big deal in the press about the window film they had just installed on the state capital building, claiming this made the windows "bullet-proof." When I saw this reported, I tracked down the politicians behind the decision and told them the window film doesn't do what they were claiming in the press.

A quick side note: If you find yourself in a similar situation and discover you've installed the wrong product or implemented an ineffective measure, then once you realize your mistake, just fix it. It really is that simple. Once you know better, fix it and move on to the next problem.

Anyway, the politicians went back to the company who had sold them the product and asked for a live demo—something they should have asked for in the first place. They discovered that I'd told them the truth about the window film and that the company had lied in their bids. Did the officials report their mistake in the media, though? Were there any articles about it? Of course not. They didn't want to admit they'd wasted taxpayer money and then lose votes. They didn't want to admit they hadn't thoroughly vetted the vendor's claims but had simply accepted a sales pitch.

We've got to push for more ethical practices in media—ones not driven by what makes money but what is in the public interest. Ones that can't be manipulated to push an agenda but to present the truth. That's the true heart of journalism—to find and share the truth. We need to reclaim this.

SCHOOL RESPONSE

Finally, I want to address how schools need to respond in the aftermath of a shooting. Those first days may feel chaotic. If you're a head administrator, you're likely getting calls from all directions—parents, other school officials, law enforcement, politicians, news outlets. It's overwhelming.

But your primary duty should be to support your staff. Make sure they can take the appropriate amount of time off afterward. You might recall earlier in the book, I mentioned how the administrators of Sandy Hook wanted staff and children back in class the following Monday, which was way too fast.

The push to "get back to normal" is often motivated by attendance-based funding. Since many states fund schools based on the number of school days they are open, money becomes the central concern instead of caring for people. Administrators feel pressured to get everyone back into class, so they don't lose funding for the next year.

However, even in these states, there is always an allowance of exception days for unexpected school closures, like inclement weather. What we need is a governor's directive to override the funding issue so affected schools are granted additional exception days. After all, even if you have staff who were not in the attacked school, people across the district will have funerals to attend and trauma to deal with. Exceptions should be based on the scale of devastation from the shooting.

As the head of the school, it's your job to reach out to the state and insist on an exception so your people can adequately grieve. Be the advocate for your staff and students and insist on the time off without any impact to your funding. If the state fights back, well, then that's a great time to contact a politician or the media to make some noise. At least your people will know you're fighting for their needs.

Meanwhile, network with other schools in adjacent districts. Can students from the affected school join their classes for an interim period? This is especially important in the investigation and cleanup phase. Also, it may be easier for a traumatized student to get back to school in a different environment than having to immediately walk right back into the room where they witnessed horrific violence.

Reach out to local counseling centers, churches, temples, and so on to see if they can provide additional therapeutic and pastoral support. In the aftermath of a shooting, many schools only rely on their one school counselor who may not be equipped for handling this specific type of trauma. They easily become overwhelmed.

And let's face it—you are going to be overwhelmed, too. After going to over sixty active shooter scenes, I've seen the overwhelm and guilt in school leaders in those first days. Based on what I've seen to be effective, here are some best practices for you in the aftermath:

- Immediately after, work with law enforcement to help them ID the victims and make sure the building is clear. LEOs and EMTs won't know your building as well as you do, so the sooner you can help them find everyone, the sooner they can get medical care, be reunited with parents, or in the case of death, the family can be notified.

- After an appropriate time of grieving, don't rush back to "normal" schedules. Instead, try a couple of half-days of classes to see how things go and gauge the mood of both staff and students. Then, you can better determine how to move forward, whether more half-days or returning to a regular full schedule.

- Make sure you give people time to grieve in whatever way they need. For some kids, they want to stand where their friends died and set up a memorial. If that's what they need, then let them so they can process through the pain.

- Recognize things will never be the same again.

This was something that came up in a conversation I had with Kaitlin Roig-DeBellis, a Sandy Hook teacher who protected fifteen of her students on the day of the attack and has gone on to found the nonprofit Classes 4 Classes, Inc.

"[The trauma] doesn't go anywhere," she pointed out. "We're expected to 'move on' … so we need to do a better job as a whole, as a society, of helping people to understand you're not alone … that you're wholly allowed to have the feelings you're feeling … That's okay. You learn to live with it in a new way … you move forward."[28]

---

28 You can see the full interview on Armoured One's YouTube channel: https://www.youtube.com/watch?v=7-hucsSiwrl&t=490.

STAYING ONE STEP AHEAD

In a study looking at shootings between 2009 and 2016, they found that "At Sandy Hook, test results fell dramatically after the shooting,"[29] and "Chronic absenteeism at Sandy Hook Elementary more than doubled in the year after the shooting."[30] So, it should come as no surprise if your students need additional educational support as they recover.

Don't worry so much about "moving on." Instead, move forward.

MOVING FORWARD

Before we discuss trauma and PTSD more specifically, it's also worth mentioning that there is no shame in asking for help. Uvalde is an underprivileged district, but they have begun to rebuild, thanks to various organizations who have stepped up to donate and offer their support to the city's recovery.

A prime example is the Texas grocery chain H-E-B that has donated $10 million for a new school to be built. As of June 2022, the plan is to demolish Robb Elementary and replace it with a memorial park.[31] In this way, the city can honor the lives that were lost while helping kids move forward in a new, updated school. After all, most people don't want to live in a home where a murder took place—much less go to school where so many died.

---

29 Phillip B. Levine and Robin McKnight, "Exposure to a School Shooting and Subsequent Well-Being," National Bureau of Economic Research, December 2020, NBER Working Paper No. 28307, JEL No. 118,121, accessed March 14, 2024, 12, https://www.nber.org/papers/w28307.

30 Ibid., 2.

31 Brian Lopez, "Butt Family, H-E-B Donate $10 million to Replace Robb Elementary School in Uvalde after Mass Shooting," *Texas Tribune*, June 28, 2022, accessed March 14, 2024, https://www.texastribune.org/2022/06/28/uvalde-robb-elementary-donation/.

Despite the evil we see in school shootings, there is also plenty of good in the world. If you reach out for help, you will find people willing to offer a hand. Don't feel like you have to figure it out all alone. It's why we started Armoured One. It's why I decided to write this book. We can help each other move forward—one step at a time.

7

RECOVERY

It's no understatement to say it changed the world when the World Trade Center came down on 9/11. Soon after, my dad decided to pull the family together and let us know that he was heading down to Ground Zero to serve and help. This came as no surprise to me, having watched how my dad selflessly served others as a pastor for my entire life.

He spent the next year going to Ground Zero helping victims' families and first responders, and the FBI eventually made him an official chaplain. He later told me about what they did whenever a body was found in the rubble. All construction equipment would stop, and everyone would be silent in reverence to the life lost.

My dad's approach with people was to ask how 9/11 affected them, listen, and just show them love. He never forced himself on people. Dad would simply walk up to anyone with a dead stare in their eyes or who looked like they didn't care if they took another breath. He'd place his hand on their shoulder and ask them, "Do you mind sharing with me how this affected you?"

One time, an older, retired FDNY fireman opened up about his grief—how his grandson who had followed in his footsteps had been killed when one of the jumpers landed on him, killing him instantly.

The grieving grandfather broke down and hugged my dad. He sobbed, "I wish I had one more moment with my grandson to tell him I loved him and that I was so proud of him. Why couldn't it have been me instead of my grandson?"

My dad absorbed the man's pain—and I saw it in his eyes as he shared this story with me. I could tell that my dad had been through a lot at Ground Zero—more pain than most people would ever want to experience in a lifetime.

The hardest part of my job isn't the crime scenes but meeting the victims' families and seeing the pain and the hurt in their eyes. When those parents dropped their kids off in the morning, they were expecting a normal night where their child comes home to do their homework, eat dinner, and kiss them good night as they put them to bed. Instead, they are lost in a surreal fog because their child did *not* come home.

They know they will never see them again, but their heart does not want to accept the truth. Even the parents whose child is shot but survives, part of their child dies that day, and they carry the trauma for the rest of their lives.

Once I began focusing my work on school shootings, I decided to follow my dad's lead. Whenever we arrive on the scene of a school active shooter like Uvalde or Sandy Hook, I treat it the same way my dad treated Ground Zero. The attack may be over—but the long road to recovery has just begun.

THE DEGREES AND DANGERS OF TRAUMA

Active shooter scenarios create different degrees of trauma. In recovering, we need more recognition for *all* these degrees, not just certain ones.

In my work, I've often found it's only the people who were shot and killed or shot and injured who qualify for support resources.

Likewise, the media focuses largely on the victims who were killed or injured. But what about the people who survived an attack?

The students and staff in some of these school attacks have actually been through a battle. They have watched their friends get shot and killed right next to them. These poor kids and parents in Uvalde have survived the unimaginable. They have literally witnessed more violence and death than what ninety percent of our soldiers have seen.[32] One fourth-grade girl in Uvalde survived by covering herself in her dead friend's blood and playing dead. I don't know many adults who could handle that.

The trauma is overwhelming, not only for victims who were wounded but the forgotten victims who have PTSD from the attack. The ones who were in the building or in the school district. There are families who get no help with treating their child's PTSD. We've seen some deadly results from this neglect as students have committed suicide after witnessing such horrific events.

Imagine being in fourth grade and a shooter enters your classroom with a rifle. He shoots your teacher and classmates, but you are fortunate enough to survive uninjured. You're left alone to manage the horrific memories—all while news people shove microphones in your face, asking you to relive the worst moment of your life.

Or imagine being a third grader and hearing shots in the fourth-grade classroom. Those fourth graders could be your friends who live next door, kids you looked up to. Imagine wondering if the attacker is headed to your classroom next. That kind of fear doesn't just evaporate right away.

Do you think that every student and staff member in that school was affected? Do you wonder what the impact was for every student

---

32   Everett Bledsoe, "Answering: What Percentage of the Military Sees Combat?" TheSoldiersProject.org, October 1, 2023, accessed March 12, 2024, https://www. thesoldiersproject.org/what-percentage-of-the-military-sees-combat/.

and staff member on that campus or in that district? What about the parents or family members who heard about the attack and didn't know if their child was alive? I ask only because many people do not realize just how many victims there are to these horrible attacks—especially when it comes to the lingering effects of PTSD.

I spoke to one of the victim's families in Parkland whose son was never shot and survived on the third floor of Building 12. During the attack, he attempted to run down the stairs to get out of the school and saw the shooter. He turned around, ran back to the third floor, but was locked out of his classroom. Despite this, he didn't give up and somehow got into a room and to safety. But while he was safe, he heard the shooter execute his friends and teachers.

Yes, he lived, but he fights immense survivor's guilt. Since the attack, he constantly feels like someone is trying to kill him. He never used drugs or alcohol before the attack and began using them to mask the pain. Sadly, this young, happy kid turned depressed and even attempted suicide in front of a family member. Thank God, he was saved. Yet, the state of Florida does not see him as a victim, and the family gets no help treating his PTSD.

We need to start recognizing there are many forms of victims from an active shooter attack. The friends and family members of victims from school shootings, families whose child was injured, families whose child was in the building during a shooting, or even if they are a student on that campus. To me, they're all victims.

They are not all the same type of victims, but they are all suffering with varying degrees of PTSD. They have been traumatized, and part of their lives have been taken away from them. Many of them have had their childhoods ripped away and were robbed of their innocence.

I think about this in a similar way to how we would categorize hurricanes—yes, some hurricanes cause more damage, but they are all dangerous. In my work, I've created my own system to help rate the degree of trauma, with the highest number representing the most severe to least.

As a caveat, I am not a doctor, and there is nothing overtly scientific here. But from my own therapy and personal experience with trauma and helping others with trauma, I've found this to be helpful in assisting people to recover after an active shooter incident.

MY ACTIVE SHOOTER DEGREES OF PTSD

Category 6: Parents who lost a child or a loved one. This could also include the siblings of the murdered child, grandparents, or other close family members affected directly by the child's death. Many of them will still be grappling with the loss, detachment to others, marital problems, even substance abuse issues to numb the pain.

Category 5: Victims who were shot/injured but survived the attack. This also includes their family members. Not only are they dealing with the physical pain and recovery from being injured, but many of them do not feel psychologically safe anywhere they go. Loud noises terrify them, and they keep looking over their shoulder because they feel hunted. I have met some kids grappling with survivors' guilt and even had parents tell me that they feel guilty that their child survived while their friend's kid did not. They have tremendous pain, both physically and mentally.

Category 4: These are the victims who were in the room or area of the attack. They witnessed the shooting and murders firsthand. I include their parents or loved ones in this category. These witnesses live with flashbacks of violence since they had front-row seats to the worst horror show no one should ever see. Their parents and family members are trying to help them overcome this trauma to hopefully live a normal life.

Category 3: This includes students and staff who were in the building during the attack, plus their families. I also count the local religious leaders who buried victims or are counseling the victims and families. Just because they didn't *see* the actual shooting or violence doesn't mean they are not suffering, too. Secondary trauma can easily turn into compassion fatigue and depression.

Category 2: Victims here include the rest of the school campus/district's students, staff, and parents. Every one of them has to live with the residual fear for their lives or the lives of friends and family. They had limited information during the event and did not know if someone was coming to kill them next. Parents wondered if their kids were going to come home that day—or not.

Category 1: This includes the rest of the entire community. Active shooter events cause pain, fear, and division throughout the community in the aftermath. I have watched communities tear themselves apart after a shooting because they want someone to pay for what went wrong. They demand immediate, drastic changes because they are living in a reality-based fear that this could happen again. Imagine sending your kid back to a classroom when your school district just had twenty-one people killed in a school.

When I arrived in Uvalde the day after the attack, I was the first person from our team on scene. Walking up to the school, the whole area was taped off, and you couldn't even get to the front yard. Near the Robb Elementary School sign, I saw families dropping off flowers and crying.

The grief is so incredibly strong at these shootings. The horror and nightmare these families and communities are living in is unimaginable. I'll keep saying it—as a nation, we *need* to have more recognition of this pain and ensure victims have the resources for recovery, even if they were not in the building itself.

I find myself at a loss for words after going to these shootings for over ten years. I find many Americans even become traumatized to some extent by watching the news unfold and wondering if their own kid's school will be next. Driven by fear, I see way too many schools buy products and services that will do nothing to protect kids—or as a way to quiet the more vocal parents. My heart sinks when I watch local news channels do interviews with the school superintendents saying what they did to protect their kids—and too often, what they did is worse than doing nothing.

Clearly, I'm an advocate for better school security. But we have to make wiser choices in the aftermath. Otherwise, recovery won't truly be recovery. We'll let PTSD in the driver's seat—and it's a *terrible* driver as I've seen in my own life, from my crabbiness on the morning of Uvalde to the loss of friends to suicide.

When we recognize the dangers of trauma and respond appropriately to the degree of trauma someone is experiencing, we can make real progress on the road to recovery. Only then can we do something else entirely surprising—we can use trauma for *good*.

USING PTSD FOR GOOD

Like most police officers and first responders, I suffer from my own PTSD from what I've seen. Most people suffer one way or another from PTSD—whether directly from something they've experienced firsthand or because they know someone with PTSD. When I signed up at twenty years old to become a police officer, I had no clue the true impact PTSD would have on my life. The cases of children being abused or murdered stick out in my mind more than anything else.

One such case was a homicide of a beautiful two-year-old girl where her mother's boyfriend killed her. He grabbed this little two-year-old baby by her leg and beat her into the floor like she was a hammer. This little angel was rushed into ICU where she later died. What hurts so bad is I had an opportunity to save her.

Two weeks prior to her murder, I was on patrol and called to her house on a possible child abuse case. It was reported that the two-year-old was hurting the six-month-old baby. The boyfriend had called to say the two-year-old girl was hitting the baby. We completed an investigation there and did not see any visible injuries on the six-month-old or the two-year-old girl.

Looking back, I still feel like I could have done *something* different. That poor girl was still killed, and I was left with guilt and remorse from it. If that wasn't bad enough, I had to watch the baby's mother beg the judge to *not* lock up her boyfriend who had murdered her baby. He was sentenced to less than twenty years for killing a *two-year-old*. And that's just one case of many I witnessed.

For years, I've been going to a psychologist, not only to learn how to deal with my PTSD but to also repurpose it for good. Getting counseling has made me a better detective, CEO, husband, father, and leader. It also reaffirmed why I started Armoured One. My PTSD has given me more passion to fight, more energy and vision to end the story of active shooter. If it wasn't for all I suffered through, I wouldn't be as effective.

The day after the Sandy Hook Elementary School attack, I drove to their "Ground Zero" and began my own investigation. I had no jurisdiction and didn't know if anyone would be willing to answer any of my questions. With my background in law enforcement, I walked around the scene and asked people how the attack had affected them—just like Dad had done after 9/11.

I already knew how to do a thorough investigation and how to interview people, but this time, I was not in uniform or wearing a badge. No one had to talk to me, but I quickly discovered that people were more than willing to share how they had been affected.

As I spoke with people, I discovered how bad it hurts to hear their stories and see their pain. To see them pray and be mad at God and say, "How could You let this happen? Why did You let this happen?" But I also realized how much help it brought them by being able to open up to someone who just *listened* to them. Many times, I didn't even have to say anything after I asked that first question—they just kept talking and talking.

Not only do you hear how that child they knew died, but you hear the amazing story about their life. I can relate because I still love sharing stories about my brother Jeremy who died of an unexpected heart attack at only forty-one. So far, his death is the hardest personal loss I have ever faced.

The death of your loved one is the hard part to talk about. I talk about the jokes Jeremy and I had, how he was an incredible fisherman, dad, and teacher. Sharing about his life is easier than talking about the way he died without warning.

As my dad would say at funerals, it's great to talk about "their dash." Dad referred to people's dash as that little line between their date of birth and the date of death. For Jeremy, it was 1976–2016. That little dash holds all the memories, stories, and value to that person's life. My dad always stressed that "you need to make the dash count."

When I take my collected trauma—my career in law enforcement, the losses of loved ones like my brother, and the school shootings I've been to—it has allowed me to repurpose my PTSD for good. To be able to listen to people, be there for them in the hurt, and help them begin recovery.

You can do the same. If you ever find yourself in a situation facing the aftermath of terrible loss, you can dig into your own trauma and use it to connect with those who are suffering. You can use your scars to treat their fresh wounds. And as I've learned, you often don't have to say anything special. You just have to *be* there. Make your dash count!

This is the best advice I can give to communities who are in recovery. Be there for each other. Listen to one another. Don't try to "move on" too fast. Let the feelings run their course. It hurts like heck. But it's the first step in healing.

ADVOCACY

So, what can we do to actually help in the recovery process? Beyond being there for one another and listening, what are some proactive steps we can take to help our communities?

First, start with advocacy. Speak up. Be heard. Write to your elected representatives at every level and demand specific changes. Don't settle for the surface-level statements. If you do, then you'll end up with the same situation we're seeing in Tennessee where substandard products have been given the state's blessing—which is only wasting taxpayer's money, creating a false sense of security, and doing nothing to protect their schools.

What *should* you be advocating for?

Standardized active shooter training for both schools and law enforcement. There should be minimum standards for who is allowed to conduct the training and how many hours are required annually.

Training for all staff at schools and law in enforcement. All school staff should be trained, from maintenance to the shop teacher, to the head football coach, to the part-time bus driver and substitutes. If they receive as much as a penny from your school, they need to know protocols and procedures.

The same goes for law enforcement—from the 911 operator being able to do a reverse-911 call to every LEO putting in the time every year for a hands-on, simulated response training.

Minimum standards for school building security. This includes automatic locking doors, lockdown buttons and systems, and protocols for keycards, electronic access, and limited building access.

Grants and funding for security. At Armoured One, we have access to grant writers to help schools get funding they need for additional security measures. You can push your school board and elected officials to make this standard practice for your school—create the budget for changes like a full-time SRO, updated doors, blue light systems, automated lockdown systems—and then find the funding to make it all happen.

Emergency counseling support. Earlier in the book, I mentioned how we should treat the recovery process for active shooter events the same way FEMA responds after a natural disaster. We have to do so proactively, though, by establishing a network of certified counselors, therapists, and religious leaders who are prepared to spring into action.

With so many shootings happening in small communities, they often lack these resources, but we can develop networks of counseling professionals who are "on call" for such events, ready to support communities for the year (or longer) following a shooting.

While you can and should do all these *without* a state mandate, the sooner we can advocate for these measures to be put into law and standard procedures, the sooner we can thwart the next shooter *and* help hurting communities in their recovery.

Don't wait for someone to do any of this for you. You can start today.

Because advocacy is not enough on its own, it must be paired with taking the right actions. Only then will we have true change, true protection for our children, and truly bring an end to the story of active shooter by staying one step ahead.

CONCLUSION

TAKE ACTION

Growing up, I struggled in school. Back in the 1980s and early 1990s, the schools I was in didn't recognize learning disabilities like dyslexia, so it wasn't until I was an adult I found out I had a couple forms of the condition. Looking back now, I feel bad for most of my teachers and what they had to put up with from me.

But you know what? I had some incredible teachers who helped me along the way—educators like Mrs. Brunette and Mrs. Gillespie from Baldwinsville Central Schools in New York and Mr. Rombosac and Mrs. Armstrong from Highland Falls Central Schools. These were caring, compassionate teachers who were patient with me and helped me succeed to become who I am today. They encouraged and motivated me in ways I'll always be grateful for. They understood that knowledge only matters if you can act upon it—and if you actually use it.

Throughout this book, I know I've given you a ton of information. Some of it has likely been challenging. I hope some of it has been refreshing and encouraging.

But more than anything, I hope it's been *motivating*.

Knowledge will only take you so far. It's time to take action.

Follow the advice laid out throughout this book so you take the *right* actions. Don't wait for change. *Be* the change. The government can't solve the problem for us. If they could, they'd have done it twenty-five years ago after Columbine. Also, the media isn't going to save your kids. They may help spark the conversation, but then they move on to the next "big" story.

But you can control what you do. Now, you have the knowledge to start building a more secure environment.

"But, Tom, where do we even start?"

That's a great question. Your starting line may be very different than the starting line for the next district over from you. So, to help you find the start point for you, quickly review some of the major points we've discussed throughout.

Review your training. Take a hard look at how you're training your staff. It's literally the most important action you can take to save lives. Are you using federally recognized training? Are you documenting that *everyone* is trained? Is your training creating fear or focus? Are you being trained by someone who is certified—or just a self-proclaimed expert?

Review your building security. Look at how you can harden doors, locks, and glass to create barriers for an attacker. Try to see your building the way a shooter would. Where are the vulnerabilities? How can you restrict access and slow down an attacker? How can you help law enforcement in their response? Do you have full lockdown systems in place?

Know your protectors. Build strong relationships with your local LEOs. Know who they are and how they are trained. That is, don't blindly trust them like we saw in Uvalde. Instead, hold them accountable to be trained and capable. Hire SROs who are true warriors of compassion and action. Do walk-throughs with your LEOs and have them involved in the community. This alone can dissuade many would-be shooters.

Assess threats and equip kids. While we don't advocate for full active shooter training for students, you can still equip them through drills to know how to follow directions in a way that boosts confidence. Create avenues for students to report concerns they have about their friends.

Instill a healthy culture of "see something, say something" around threats and bullying. By being proactive, we can make a difference.

Question your assumptions. Go back to chapter 2 and highlight the myths and assumptions you see happening in your school district. Use those as conversation starters among staff and with your school board, PTA, and administrators.

Review your policies and protocols. Whether you're in a school or law enforcement, take a fresh look at your policies and protocols, especially where it is related to training and response. What bad practices need to be weeded out? Is there any inconsistent language you can address? What are the training and policy gaps you can fill quickly?

Require real proof and standards. Don't take a vendor's word for it. Ask specific questions about the glass rating and what kind of damage it can sustain. Require proof beyond a demo video or a pamphlet. Ask about ASTM ratings and *be skeptical.* A good company won't be afraid of questions but will welcome them.

Review the Ten Commandments of Preparation. How many of them are you already following? Which ones do you still need to incorporate? Who can help you with preparing?

Bolster your community relationships. Look at who you know in the community who can help in a crisis: the local metro system to help with evacuating kids, organizations willing to be a secondary location for evacuation and pickup, and local counselors and religious leaders who can provide recovery support.

Made a Mistake? Look, we all make mistakes every day in life. If through this book you discovered you've done something wrong or made a mistake in your security, fix it. Don't ignore it. It will cost money, but the money is nothing compared to losing a life.

Review your communication resources. Examine how you communicate with parents and the community at large. Do you have automated messages and systems in place for emergencies? Do parents know about the social media accounts and email list? Do teachers have a way to communicate with each other (i.e., radios) and with law enforcement in the event of an attack?

If you're still not sure where to start, then give us a call. Reach out to me and the rest of the Armoured One team. Part of why I wrote this book is because we love giving people the advice and counsel they need to protect kids. That's what it's really about. So, if you're feeling overwhelmed, then let's have a conversation and make this process easier for you.

Remember, each action you take on this list makes you safer today than you were yesterday. But if you do nothing else, focus on training as it is the number one predictor of success in an attack.

See this as your opportunity to stand up and make sure things are done right. Do your research, fix your training problems, fix your security issues—just don't try to do it all alone. If you're a parent reading this, demand safety and security be the number one priority for your school board—everything from CPR training, presence of AED units, to active shooter training.

Remember, you're the ones voting board members into their positions, so they have to answer to you. Push for change. And if you don't see it, then *vote* for change. Vote for people who will prioritize safety first. Get this book for them, flag the Ten Commandments chapter, and ask, "Are you following this?"

Fight for freedom—our children's freedom but also the freedom of our children's children. The more correct actions we take, the more unified we are around prioritizing safety, the more demoralizing it will be for would-be shooters. When they see these changes happening, they'll lose confidence they can just walk in and destroy. Better yet, they may wake up and seek the help they really need instead of turning to a gun.

Today, I have six children of my own—Bailey, Noah, Isaiah, McKenzie, Adalis, and Liam. Like any good parent, I want the best educational opportunities for them. I want them to go off to a college or a trade school and have a great future pursuing their dreams and making a difference in the world.

But none of those dreams will come true if they're killed at school. There is nothing but death and destruction behind those bullets when an active shooter comes into a school. Their dreams and aspirations to go off to Yale, Harvard, or West Point can't come true if they go to school and become another name on another news report. It's why I take my work as seriously as I do—because I know every good parent out there feels the same. I'm sure *you* feel the same.

After eleven years of fighting with politicians and school districts to see change, believe me, I know how discouraging this can feel. But let me leave you with hope, because we *are* seeing change happen. From my estimation, I'm seeing a 10 percent improvement in how schools are preparing and protecting compared to ten years ago—and about a 50 percent improvement among law enforcement.

People are starting to listen. They are starting to realize the only way off this insanity cycle is to get their hands dirty and *do* the work. People are waking up to see that the only solution to this deadly déjà vu is to learn from the experts and follow their expertise—not just guessing or going through the motions.

Let's take steps together that will keep us one step ahead. With enough steps, we can end the story of active shooter. Maybe not in our lifetime, but we can put into motion the changes that will impact future generations. The pen is in our hands. We can write a new story. One of safety and security, love and compassion, where young minds can thrive because they know their bodies are safe. Why not start writing that story together?

PHOTO
GALLERY

This is my go-bag for school shootings. Everything is ready to go except for my laptop, which I grabbed.

(Uvalde) Media presence at ground zero.

(Uvalde) Another image of media at ground zero.

(Uvalde) Equipment used during Uvalde coverage.

(Uvalde) Anderson Cooper from CNN was a very nice guy who seemed very genuine about his concern for Uvalde.

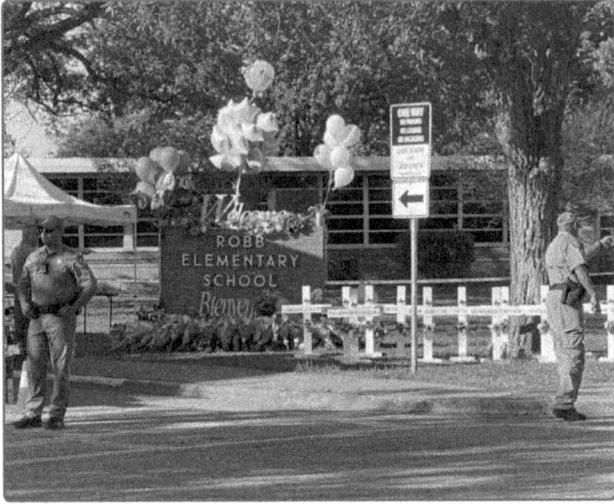

(Uvalde) This photo is the key shot the media was looking and paying for. The media paid homeowners to stand in their yards to report on the incident. We heard that one of the national news networks was paying a homeowner $10,000 a week to use his front yard. They were there for over ten weeks.

(Inside Robb Elementary, Uvalde) This hallway is where the intruder gained entry to rooms 111 and 112, which I visited approximately two months after the incident. These sturdy, hollow metal doors in the hallway could have potentially saved lives had the school possessed adequate security measures. The doors are highly resistant to breach attempts by an attacker. Ideally, they should have been pre-locked and integrated with the lockdown system to automatically release from the magnetic hold-open fire system and close during all lockdown situations. Such a setup would have provided an additional layer of defense, potentially impeding or preventing the intruder from reaching the classrooms.

(Inside Robb Elementary, Uvalde) This is the state of rooms 111 and 112 after the police completed processing the scene. The rooms were sealed off to deter looters and thrill-seekers from gaining access.

(Uvalde) One of my many visits back to ground zero.

(Uvalde) My contractor badge allowed me to help the school with its security assessment of the district after the shooting.

Uvalde's first homecoming football game following the attack. A team of individuals from Armoured One and Huckabee Architects attended the game together to offer support and aid in restoring a sense of normalcy. Although the Coyotes were defeated that night, it was a fantastic experience to witness their performance.

(Uvalde) David Muir from ABC World News on site the day after the shooting. You can see where they unscrewed the stop sign to move it and get a better view of the school behind the news anchor.

(Uvalde) The shooter's grandfather, Rolando, and I. The shooter was living with his grandfather before the attack. Rolando and his wife are victims of this shooting, and I do not blame them at all. He is a wonderful man.

www.ingramcontent.com/pod-product-compliance
Lightning Source LLC
Chambersburg PA
CBHW031434270326
41930CB00007B/703